BEHIND THE LINES
THE UNTOLD STORIES OF THE CINCINNATI RIOTS

For Marie:
Happy birthday!
and many returns.
I hope you enjoy
this.

Jeff W Bronson

BEHIND THE LINES

**BEHIND THE LINES OF ACTION, BETWEEN THE LINES OF TRUTH:
THE UNTOLD STORIES OF THE CINCINNATI RIOTS**

PETER BRONSON

CHILIDOG PRESS
MILFORD, OH

For further information, contact the publisher at:

Chilidog Press
PMB 182 - 1081-B State Route 28
Milford, OH 45150-2199

ISBN: 0-9740602-1-6

Cover design by Steve Sullivan
Cover photo by Michael E. Keating
Interior design by Angela Wilcox

Use of photos—courtesy of The Cincinnati Enquirer
 Ernest Coleman
 Glenn Hartong
 Stephen M. Herppich
 Michael E. Keating
 Gary Landers
 Craig Ruttle
 Brandi Stafford

This book is dedicated to the brave
Cincinnati Police officers
who risk their lives to keep us safe;

to everyone who reaches across the artificial
racial borders that separate God's children;

and with gratitude for the love and
encouragement of two women who never
doubted that I would write books someday:
my mother
and
my fourth-grade teacher, Miss Green.

Cops lined up in front of City Hall on April 10, as council members and city workers were told to stay inside City Hall behind locked doors.

INTRODUCTION

For a long and terrifying week in April 2001, Cincinnati, Ohio erupted in rioting. Exactly five months later to the day, lingering race problems were shoved off the front pages by the shocking terrorist attacks on September 11. That put the city's riots in harsh perspective. Compared to what happened at the World Trade Center in New York, Cincinnati's "unrest" was like a domestic dispute in the middle of a natural disaster.

But the two events had something in common: five years later, the immediate impact of both had faded like yellowed headlines in an attic. All the stirring vows of unity and emotional calls to action were mostly forgotten—except by the people who had been directly involved in the trenches, who could not forget or "move on."

To those who experienced the riots, the sounds, smells, sights and vivid memories were still as real as the eye-stinging smoke that filtered through the streets during that unseasonably balmy springtime week.

I watched the riots on CNN, more than a thousand miles away, while on vacation in Florida. It was like watching a well-respected good friend suddenly show up on the news, doing something bizarre, outrageous and completely out of character, like holding up a bank or shooting it out with police. I could not believe those scenes of looting and beatings were from the streets of polite, family-friendly Cincinnati.

By April 16, when I got back to my office at the *Enquirer* where I was editorial page editor at the time, I found a city in panic, shaken by fear, eager to offer programs, spending, jobs and earnest dialogue—almost anything to make it all go away. I found a city that acted like a victim of domestic violence. It blamed the cops, made excuses for the violent abusers and refused to press charges in the court of public opinion. The race riots quickly became "unrest" or even "rebellion," suggesting rational reasons for people to break windows and beat strangers.

Business leaders called emergency meetings to promise immediate spending and jobs. The mayor announced a commission to address the root causes of the riots and called for federal investigations of the police. City Council scrambled to approve a $4.5 million settlement for a flimsy racial profiling lawsuit and squelched any objections to pacify protesters who packed their meetings.

There were exceptions. Hamilton County Prosecutor Mike Allen said he would throw the book at the rioters. "They are law-breaking thugs who should be prosecuted vigorously," he said. "That will not be tolerated in this community."

City Councilman Phil Heimlich stood up almost alone against the profiling settlement, pointing out that the city's law staff had advised that the case against the city was flawed and weak, and the city should fight it. "There was talk up here today that this was caused by social problems," he said after one council meeting to discuss the riots. "To me, that suggests excusing that kind of violence."

But Heimlich was told to sit down and be quiet. Most city leaders acted as if comments like Allen's and Heimlich's were rude violations of an unwritten code, something to be publicly ignored and privately deplored.

Meanwhile, the local media, led by *The Cincinnati Enquirer*, set aside neutral objectivity and took a leading role in playing host and organizer for community dialogue to air racial grievances. Stories about the riots and the aftermath were as thick as confetti, but nobody pasted all the pieces together to see what the big picture looked like.

What happened that week in April 2001 was the worst race rioting in Cincinnati since 1968, and the worst in America since the Rodney King case set Los Angeles aflame 10 years earlier in 1991. By the time it was over, 600 people had been arrested. The cost to the city was estimated at $14 million in direct and long-term damages. In addition to damaged city buildings, 120 businesses had been torched, looted or trashed.

A racial boycott of Cincinnati that was energized by the riots caused more damage to the city's economy and morale, as shows were canceled by Bill Cosby, Whoopi Goldberg, Wynton Marsalis and Smokey Robinson. And as part of the settlement of the racial profiling lawsuit, the city signed a collaborative agreement that put a federal monitor and a federal judge in charge of oversight of the Cincinnati Police Division, at a cost estimate of more than $10 million.

No dollar figures can measure the suffering and loss caused by an epidemic of homicides that followed the riots. More than 70 young black men were killed each year since 2001. In 2005, Cincinnati had 79 homicides, the worst annual total since 1971. Nearly all were drug related. Nearly all were black men killed by black men. The lasting legacy of the riots is more than 300 funerals for young black men.

All of that has been scattered through hundreds of headlines and news stories. But the complete story has not been told. All the scattered pieces of the puzzle have never been assembled.

Somebody needs to write this down, I thought in the years after the riots. But nobody did. So I began interviewing and collecting research in January 2004.

By then, some stories conflicted and some memories were beginning to fray at the edges. But wherever I went, people were eager to tell what happened, glad to finally have a chance to go back and set the record straight. Many openly wondered why nobody had asked them before. In many cases, key players were finally distant enough from that frantic week in April to take down the protective crime-scene tape and openly, for the first time, discuss things that had never been reported. In interviews and research, I found many untold stories of what happened on the streets, in private meetings and in boardrooms while the riots raged.

I hope this book helps Cincinnati remember what some people would probably rather forget. I hope it brings to light for the first time a dramatic story that was overlooked by the media—the heroism of the police who saved the city without firing one deadly round of live ammunition. I hope it brings to light lessons that could be critically useful to help other cities avoid someday erupting in riots. And I hope that years from now, when people wonder what madness seized Cincinnati during that hot week in April 2001, they can find some of the answers here.

As a starting point, I found it helps to have a time-line to summarize the major events:

Saturday, April 7: Timothy Thomas, 19, wanted on more than a dozen warrants, ran from police and was shot at about 2:20 a.m. in a dark alley in Over-the-Rhine by Cincinnati Police Officer Stephen Roach. The cop was white. Thomas was black and unarmed.

Sunday April 8: The first newspaper report of the incident used the words "excessive force" in the lead paragraph. It also quoted protesters from the Black United Front who accused the police of brutality, and a quote from Thomas's girlfriend calling the police "trigger happy." The police offered no explanation, held no press conference about the shooting and were not quoted. Police Chief Thomas Streicher, driving back from meetings in Indianapolis, learned of the shooting for the first time almost by accident, and was stunned and angered to learn that nobody in the Police Division had informed him or made a public statement.

Monday April 9: A meeting of the Law and Public Safety Committee at City Hall exploded in a chaos of screaming and shouting, as hundreds of protesters packed the room and took over. The chairman of the meeting, Councilman John Cranley, was pushed and shoved when he tried to call a recess to use a restroom, and the leader of the Black United Front, the Rev. Damon Lynch III, told council members they would not be allowed to leave until they provided answers.

Windows at City Hall were smashed as the crowd left to gather in front of Police Headquarters. The mob swelled to more than 1,000 and began throwing rocks and bottles at police, who responded with mounted horses, then dispersion gas and beanbag shotguns.

Tuesday April 10: Rioting became more violent. The first casualties were reported, including an elderly couple that was dragged from their car and beaten severely. Firefighters were swamped by calls and refused to get out of their trucks without police protection. An FBI investigation into the shooting of Thomas was announced. City Council canceled its scheduled weekly meeting. Lynch called for a Peace Walk that slipped out of control and turned into a violent confrontation with police. Rioters broke car windshields and store windows and burned and looted businesses.

Wednesday April 11: Probably the worst day of rioting. Violence spread beyond crime-ridden Over-the-Rhine to several residential neighborhoods—Avondale, Bond Hill, Madisonville, Roselawn, Corryville and Evanston. Shops were burned. Motorists were dragged from cars and beaten in blocked intersections. Rioters tried to march to Fountain

Square in the downtown business district, but police formed a wall along Central Parkway. The rioters charged; police held their ground and pushed them back by firing beanbag shotguns.

A group of black ministers, led by Cincinnati Human Relations Director Cecil Thomas, formed a human chain between the rioters and police to turn the violent youths back. Late that night, as police hunted for a rooftop sniper, a cop was shot by a man in the crowd. The bullet was deflected by his belt buckle and he was not injured.

Thursday, April 12: Cincinnati Mayor Charlie Luken declared a state of emergency, asked for help from 75 State Highway Patrol officers and announced a curfew from 8 p.m. to 6 a.m.

The city braced for more rioting, but the curfew surprisingly worked. After arresting 66 rioters the day before, police arrested 136 for curfew violations and the violence subsided.

Good Friday, April 13: The first day of relative peace. The Fraternal Order of Police responded to protesters and news stories that had been repeating the widespread accusation that 15 black men had been killed by police. FOP President Keith Fangman pointed out that most of the suspects killed in confrontations with police had been armed, some had shot at officers and all of them had been resisting arrest. "Our police officers are not some band of rogue Nazis roaming Cincinnati hunting down and killing black men," Fangman said. "That is inflammatory. It is racist and it is wrong."

Saturday, April 14: The funeral for Timothy Thomas at Lynch's church in Over-the-Rhine drew hundreds inside and hundreds more outside on the street. Ordered to clear an intersection of protesters, a police team moved in and fired beanbag rounds into a crowd. News reports said the shots were unprovoked and without warning. The police officers said they warned the unruly crowd and had no other choice to clear the intersection to prevent more violence and beatings.

Easter Sunday, April 15: The day was peaceful, the curfew was lifted.

Monday, April 16: City council's meeting was packed with protesters again, and council members rushed to approve a settlement of a class-action racial profiling lawsuit by the Black United Front and the ACLU. A federal investigation of the Beanbag incident was launched; nearly a year later, the "Beanbag Six" officers were exonerated and the city finally reimbursed their legal expenses.

Rioters overturned a hotdog stand and pelted the vendor with soda cans on Main Street near the county courthouse as they went through Over-the-Rhine smashing windows and setting fires on April 10.

CHAPTER 1

SHOOTING AND SHOWDOWN

Easter came early that year, as if the Resurrection was impatient, pushing its way past the lingering snows of March like early daffodils.

Spring was in a hurry too. It seemed to skip its own slow overture and fast-forward to the final act of late June. Spring break emptied the schools, and kids poured out of classrooms that were still stale with the bottled-up breath of winter. They ran headlong through heavy school doors into sudden summertime.

Bankers and lawyers strolled down Fourth Street carrying suit jackets like pelts over their shoulders, sweating through buttoned-down shirts and scratchy wool slacks, taking their sweet time on the way back from lunch as if they were dawdling at recess, trying to ignore the ringing school bell.

Kids peeled off their hooded sweatshirts and official NFL Merchandise jackets and left them scattered all over playgrounds and parks like the cast-off burdens of winter's retreating army. In the stuffy upper floors of old red-brick apartments with paint-sealed grimy windows that looked down on Vine Street and Elm Street, north of Central Parkway, moms on the system went looking for the free window fans that were handed out at the Food Bank during the big heat wave the previous July. In time they gave up against the crowding heat and went down dark, littered wooden stairways, past graffiti and gouged walls, guided by sagging railings to the bright street below.

There in the warm sunshine, they sat on the steps and watched the traffic go by in a giddy rush of spring fever as if it couldn't wait to leave them and their poverty behind.

Seventy-five degrees in the first week of April was too much. All the bottled-up energy and frustration of a long and cold winter blew the cap off Cincinnati, and the whole jar of wintery gray January restlessness was tipped over into the streets. The heat caught the city by surprise, like a dough-faced tourist climbing off a plane in tropical Tampa, still wearing a turtleneck wool sweater and the surprised expression of someone who can't quite believe the steamy heat.

Cincinnati was hot that first week of April, 2001. But it was about to get a lot hotter in ways that thermometers can't measure and meteorologists can't predict. Almost nobody saw it coming.

The official version was that the meltdown began a few hours before dawn at about 2:15 a.m. on Saturday, April 7, when Timothy Thomas, 19, wanted on more than a dozen warrants, took off running when he was spotted by a cop outside a nightclub in the poverty-pocket neighborhood known as Over-the-Rhine. Officer Stephen Roach, working alone that night, was among several cops who responded for backup. He jumped out of his cruiser and ran down a dark alley to intercept the fleeing suspect, then shot Thomas as he burst around a corner and reached down to pull up his drooping pants. Roach said he thought Thomas was reaching for a gun. On a police map that marked gunshots with black pins, the alley where Thomas was shot, at Republic and 13th, would be marked by a dark cluster of pins like feeding flies. Cops called it a shooting gallery, one of the most dangerous streets in the city, behind enemy lines where drug gangs ruled at night and only the brave, stupid, lost or heavily armed wandered during daylight.

÷÷÷

In media accounts, that shooting "triggered the riots." But riots did not begin that night or the next morning, or even the morning after that. The shooting of Thomas only shook up the bottle. What really blew the lid off was a confrontation at City Hall two days later, when civil rights lawyer Ken Lawson demanded answers and the boss of the Black United Front boycott, the Rev. Damon Lynch III, barred the doors, threatened city council members and told them "Nobody leaves" until Thomas's mother got an explanation about the shooting. The pandemonium that followed broke the seal on a pressurized container of violence, as protesters shouted obscenities at council members, climbed on tables and trapped the political leaders of Cincinnati in their own council chambers.

Then there's the "root causes" media version of What Really

Happened. It would never be reported in so many words of white guilt, but the sharp edges poked through nearly every story about that week in April, harder to hide than an ax in a lunch bag. According to the TV stations and newspapers, Cincinnati was a neglected warehouse of dry-rot bigotry, packed to the ceilings with tinderbox grudges and racial animosity, just waiting for a stray spark to set off the flames. According to the root-causes explanation, what happened was not race riots, looting, beatings and wild thuggery—it was a justifiable aggravated assault on years of racist insults and police oppression, by a mob with pitchforks and torches, beating down the doors of the Queen City castle of white rule. In the media, the race riots became "rebellion" or "unrest."

But cops who were out in the streets tell another story. They say the riots that beat Cincinnati to its knees for a week actually began two days after Thomas was shot, on the afternoon and evening of April 9, right after the mob takeover of City Hall, just a few blocks away at the First District Police Headquarters.

÷ ÷ ÷

When the protesters finally filtered out of City Hall and spilled into the streets that Monday afternoon, the angry crowd began to inhale raw emotional energy the way a hurricane sucks up hot, humid air and gathers wind velocity. By the time it reached police headquarters, the mob had swelled by hundreds and word was spreading fast on the streets of Over-The-Rhine and the West End, pulling in bored, out-of-school black kids like an electron magnet.

Resembling a shoe box, the First District Police Headquarters building is long and rectangular, with large squarish blue-tinted windows set in light beige brick. It looks more like a 1950s high school than the nearly windowless Taft High School next door. But there was no doubt which was the police building on April 9, 2001. About two dozen cops were waiting along the street, directly in front of the building on Ezzard Charles Drive, which was named after Cincinnati's most famous heavyweight prizefighter. The cops lined up along the sidewalk, stood in the hot sun and watched the crowd swell to more than 1,000, like a fast-growing deadly organism, all arms and legs and shouting heads. Rocks and bottles began to fly through the air at them, shattering on the sidewalk and bouncing off the walls of the First District Headquarters behind them.

There was a loud crash as a police station window was shattered by a rock. Several cops made a move forward, preparing to wade into the crowd and grab the man who threw it. But they were stopped. Assistant Police Chief Ron Twitty, the ranking officer in charge, ordered them to back off and let him go.

"He came over the radio and said 'Do not go get him,'" recalled Officer John Rose.

Instead, Twitty sent someone for a bullhorn. As the uniform officers stood there, battered by waves of insults and stones, they began to hope that finally, someone was going to take charge and order the mob to disperse. Surely Twitty would read them the genuine riot act, they thought, and tell them to go home or go to jail. He would call in reinforcements in riot gear, deploy tear gas, and bring in the mounted division.

Twitty was in the right place at the right moment. A round man with a round face and eager, friendly smile, in his neatly pressed uniform and white hat he looked like just the strong commander the situation desperately needed. But that was an illusion. Twitty was not popular among many of the cops on the street that day. They did not respect him. Some thought he had only been promoted to fill race quotas, not on the merits of his own abilities or test scores.

Ron Twitty was the highest ranking black officer in Cincinnati Police history, the first black Lieutenant Colonel. In the black community, he was the cop who could be trusted, who understood the grievances, frustration and anger of living black in a city where racial friction stung like gravel in a skinned knee that never healed.

He was good at playing the role, walking the narrow line between "us" and "them." On WDBZ or WCIN, the local black talk radio stations, he would playfully indulge callers' wild speculation and high-octane rumors about the police without objection or denial, as if by merely failing to confirm them he was doing more than enough to set the record straight. He was used as a photo-op prop for ribbon cuttings and official visits when a high-ranking black face was needed. His personnel file was stuffed with thank-you notes from social service and civil rights groups. Twitty was genuinely liked, even loved by many in the community, but he had carved out a role more like official greeter and "community liaison" than like a potential police chief.

But that's what many outside the police division believed was in his future: first black police chief of Cincinnati. In reality, it was a stretch that could not be reached even by the elastic congeniality of the very likeable Ron Twitty.

On that fateful hot April day, while the afternoon sun slanted across a mob that pulled down the U.S. flag at the police memorial across the street, stepped on it, spit on it and raised it again upside down over a granite monument that listed all the names of the Cincinnati officers who had given their lives to protect the city, Ron Twitty was accidentally in charge.

Police Chief Thomas Streicher was busy, attending an emergency meeting with the city manager, then tending to stricken city Safety Director Kent Ryan, who was dizzy, pallid and short of breath. Ryan began to have heart-attack symptoms during the wild meeting at City Hall that day, falling ill during the city's worst public safety crisis since 1979, when 11 kids were trampled to death at a rock concert by the Who. As safety director, Ryan was the "firewall" between the police chief and city council, a position designed by the city charter to protect the police division from political manipulation. As Ryan struggled for breath, Streicher took him home and called an ambulance.

So it was up to Twitty. If anyone could do it, Twitty was the man to slowly twist open the bottle cap and let just enough pressure hiss out to prevent an explosion of foaming rage and broken glass.

But behind that blue line of cops, there was another version of Ron Twitty. To many of his fellow officers, especially among white cops, he was the untouchable and unaccountable teacher's pet of court-ordered affirmative action.

To them, Twitty was the most visible example of blacks who leapfrogged over white cops who had higher scores on promotion tests. He was the symbol of minority quotas in a 1981 court-ordered consent decree.

It was also an open secret in "carpetland" on the top command floors of police headquarters that Twitty was skating on the edges of trouble and might have already fallen through if not for his valuable and visible role as the city's highest ranking black officer.

He was a symbol among black officers, too. To his longtime friend and former street-patrol partner, Cecil Thomas, Twitty was a survivor who persevered to overcome a culture of racism in the police division. To Thomas and others in the association of black cops, the Sentinels, Twitty's success was a vindication and moral victory for all the black cops who were held down.

Thomas, a soft-spoken man who looks a lot younger than 53, left the Cincinnati Police to become director of the city's Human Relations Commission. He believes he had no choice. He was among the three black officers who filed the original Equal Employment Opportunity Commission complaint that led to a lawsuit and the ultimate federal consent decree that ordered the department to hire more blacks and women. At that time in 1980, about seven percent of the nearly 1,000 CPD officers were black. The court order set goals of 24 percent and 34 percent, to get closer to the 40 percent black population of Cincinnati. That meant one in every four promotions had to be a black cop, no matter what the seniority rankings and test scores said.

Many white cops were outraged when their promotions were delayed or denied to fill a quota. Black cops were just as angry at the way the bureaucracy found new ways to block them.

"Most African-Americans were being kept from promotions by their supervisors' ratings. It was the same with job assignments," Thomas said. "I was a pretty good law officer. One time I was called in to take a look at my monthly report. I was told I was doing a good job, but I needed more vice arrests. So I said, 'Just put me in old clothes and I will blend right in. I can get lots of vice arrests.' My supervisor said, 'I would, but nobody who is African-American will qualify to be in any special unit in my district.' I guess I was glad he was honest about it, because it inspired me to file the EEOC complaint that resulted in a consent decree."

After that, Thomas went through a hell of hazing and hostility from other cops, he said. "The decree opened doors, but other doors closed."

Thomas was afraid he would not get backup if he got in a jam. "I sure didn't want to find out," he said. Black cops who were promoted were disrespected and called "affirmative action" sergeants. Lists that would have put black officers in line for promotions were allowed to expire, so they would start over at the bottom again. Thomas said white sergeants were traditionally assigned to veteran cops, as mentors to show them the ropes. "Black sergeants were just thrown on the streets with no help."

White officers point to Cincinnati's history of hiring and promoting black police officers since the early 1900s. But Thomas says, "There's a culture that has been there a long time. It was there in the 60s and it's still there today. If you want to get anywhere, you have to be part of the culture. It was clearly racism."

From one side, Twitty symbolized a victory over racism. From the other, he was an unpopular race-quota colonel.

When Twitty walked out to take command in the most critical Cincinnati police crisis since the courthouse-burning race riots more than a century earlier, he was already a symbol of the deep racial divisions in his department and city. And that was just the beginning.

Among cops who sooner or later sort through nearly all the dirty sheets in a city's laundry basket, it was well known that Twitty was not getting his work done, and other cops were assigned to do it for him. His evaluation from 1998 said:

"Ron brings to the Command Staff two needed qualities—the perspective of the African-American and the 'pulse' of the community. His strength lies in his ability to relate to the community—particularly the minority community, and to people in general. His people skills will carry him a long way in his assignment. He needs to develop his administrative skills, particularly in the area of report review."

And there was another problem that did not show up in the reviews: Twice, Twitty had damaged his city-issued cars, but filed no reports. On one occasion, he tried to cover it up by taking his Ford cruiser to a body shop himself. A year later, in the summer of 2002, a similar falsified accident cut short his career.

÷ ÷ ÷

While the nervous, outnumbered cops stood waiting in the sun, while the bottles and rocks flew at them, Twitty sent for a bullhorn, then stood there waiting as the crowd kept building and the violence edged closer to the invisible mob-moment when a protest crosses the border into a riot.

Twitty took the bullhorn and put in fresh batteries to make sure it was working properly. Then, as cops watched in disbelief, he handed it over to the loudest shouter in the mob.

"There was a group there that claimed that if they had a bullhorn, they could calm people down and get them to leave," he explained later. "They tried to stop the violence, but they were shouted down by the rest of the crowd."

During the Rodney King riots in Los Angeles in 1992, there was a critical delay in police response. Post-riot analysis found that fires, property damage and many injuries might have been prevented if the police had moved in harder, faster—but the Los Angeles Police had been crippled by doubt and handcuffed by accusations of racism. Political correctness proved to be fatal for some riot victims in L.A.

Ten years later, Lieutenant Colonel Ron Twitty tried to appease a rock-throwing mob with the politically correct tactics of "dispute resolution." Let them vent. They just want to be heard. Never mind the flying rocks, shattered glass and broken laws. Give them a bullhorn.

Maybe Twitty had the right idea that day. Maybe if cops had pushed their way into the crowd to arrest the first member of the mob after the first broken window, it would have only made things worse. Maybe. But it's hard to imagine what could have been worse than what followed.

Later, when Chief Streicher arrived, darkness had fallen and the street in front of Police Headquarters was a scene from a nightmare. "There was a huge crowd out front, the windows were busted out, they had busted out the front door," Streicher said. "I saw Twitty standing there while this guy has his bullhorn, and I'm like, 'What?!' And he just has this big smile on his face. The cops were furious. I went up on the roof and said to myself, that's about enough of this."

Many cops who were there still think what Twitty did was a ridiculous joke: Here, take this bullhorn so you can amplify your insults and profanities at the police. Go ahead, use it to get more organized, so you can spread out and flood the streets with arson, looting and beatings.

Here, take this symbol of police authority and turn it over to the mob—just to show how sensitive and politically correct you are.

You could say it was a warped version of affirmative action for lawless rioters. Affirmative action put Twitty in command at a critical moment. Affirmative action quotas kept him there even after he had made mistakes that would probably get any other cop demoted or fired. And the same affirmative action thinking put a police bullhorn in the hands of an angry mob, sending a signal louder than the crash of breaking glass that the cops were going to be held back and do nothing.

The rioting that followed nearly wrecked a great city. During the weekend after the April 7 Timothy Thomas shooting the city simmered. But after the confrontations at City Hall and the Police headquarters on Monday, it erupted. The angry crowd marched to police headquarters, then stormed through the city to Republic Street where the shooting occurred, shouting, turning over news racks and trash cans along the way. Then the mob circled back to the police station. After Chief Streicher arrived, police on horses pushed the crowd back. The first beanbag shotguns were fired, along with eye-stinging clear-out gas. Twitty told the *Cincinnati Post* that the end of the peace occurred at 3 p.m. when the crowd filled up City Hall. According to some cops, the real riots began a few hours later when rocks and bottles started flying and the police window was broken. Whatever time is used, Monday, April 9 was the day violence and lawlessness spread through the city like a contagious infection.

The riots were not caused by Ron Twitty. Even his mistake would have been harmless if not for a Rodney King climate of cop-o-phobia that was carefully cultivated by a handful of instigators, tolerated by scared council members and fanned by the media.

But what if?

"If we would've gone in and told them to disperse and made arrests with a huge show of strength, the riots wouldn't have happened," said SWAT Team cop John Rose, who was on the blue line at police headquarters that day. "There were no consequences for their actions, and they could see that. It just made it worse."

Other cops who were there that day nodded in agreement.

The worst riots in America since the Rodney King riots of 1992 were out of the bottle—in a peaceful Midwestern city known for heartland values and strong law and order. Of all places, the explosion happened right in front of police headquarters—and the fuse had been lit in the city's Law and Public Safety Committee.

Councilman John Cranley (center, tie
and jacket) presided over the Law and
Public Safety meeting on April 9 that
quickly slipped into shouting protests
which led to rioting.

CHAPTER 2

LAWLESS AT PUBLIC SAFETY

"LADIES AND GENTLEMEN . . . LADIES AND GENTLEMEN . . .
LADIES AND GENTLEMEN . . . LADIES AND GENTLEMEN . . .
LADIES AND GENTLEMEN . . . LADIES AND GENTLEMEN . . .
LADIES AND GENTLEMEN . . . LADIES AND GENTLEMEN . . .
LADIES AND GENTLEMEN . . . LADIES AND GENTLEMEN . . .
LADIES AND GENTLEMEN . . . LADIES AND GENTLEMEN . . .
LADIES AND GENTLEMEN . . . LADIES AND GENTLEMEN . . .
LADIES AND GENTLEMEN . . . LADIES AND GENTLEMEN . . . "

Nearly three hours into the worst day in the long and proud history of Cincinnati City Council meetings, Councilman Jim Tarbell was trying to break through the chaos and wedge a foot in the door of sanity with a firm, polite, persistent knock, knock, knock.

"LADIES AND GENTLEMEN . . . LADIES AND GENTLEMEN . . . LADIES AND GENTLEMEN . . . LADIES AND GENTLEMEN . . . LADIES AND GENTLEMEN . . . "

It was not working. It was like trying to reason with a tornado. The mob was having none of it.

Sweat began to trickle down his nose onto his purple and silver bowtie, blue shirt and black vest. But Tarbell kept on knocking. You had to hand it to him. The guy had guts. The whole room around him looked like it could be the stage set for one of those Irwin Allen disaster movies from the 1970s: "Towering Airport Earthquake Inferno."

Council members sat at modest tables like vendors at a convention or panelists at a symposium, backlit by stunning stained-glass windows that depicted the seals of Ohio and the Northwest Ordinance. The council chambers are on the third floor of the 1893 City Hall, at the top of three flights of foot-worn marble steps in a room that is usually a quiet sanctuary of motions, seconds, "ayes," "nays" and routine Roberts Rules of Order.

But today it looked like a movie set with a cast of thousands, all screaming in hysteria in a cavernous room packed with politicos and protesters, trapped on the high ledges of racial panic, surrounded by lunatics, blinded by the eye-stinging smoke of confusion, with no way out.

They didn't listen to Tarbell. They only stopped shouting and screaming long enough to hear from a well-dressed lawyer playing Ringmaster at the City Hall Circus, who knew little and pretended he didn't know even that much.

Only Tarbell knew a possible escape path out of this imploding meeting. And nobody could hear him even if they desperately tried to listen.

÷÷÷

He was an unlikely looking hero. Back in the hippie '60s and '70s, when he was a rock promoter booking the Allman Brothers at his Ludlow Garage near the University of Cincinnati campus, Tarbell woke up one morning and inexplicably began shedding his hair. If God alone knows the number of hairs on everyone's head, then everyone knows the number on Tarbell. It's zero. No eyebrows, no beard, no hair at all. If he put on an earring and eye-patch, he could be a convincing South Seas pirate. In his bowtie and black vest, he looked like Mr. Clean's little brother who stayed off the steroids.

When Cincinnati celebrates the city's unique traditional baseball holiday to kick off the first game of the Cincinnati Reds season with Open Day parades, Tarbell is a crowd favorite, pushing a vending cart of hot peanuts in a tuxedo and top hat, honoring a legendary local character as well known as Pete Rose and Johnny Bench: "Peanut Jim."

Less well known is that Tarbell was also a descendant of the legendary early 1900s muckraking investigative reporter, Ida Tarbell, who put sand in the Rockefellers' gas tank with her book about the biggest Monopoly game in the country, "The History of the Standard Oil Company."

Tarbell was known as a man who loves his city more than some men love their own wife and kids. When he was still the gregarious and popular owner of Arnold's, one of the city's oldest saloons, he would drag out an old trombone, screw the bell to the slide, plug in a mouthpiece and play the Happy Birthday song for his friends and favorite customers. But then in the 1990s he had to sell Arnold's to pay for his Quixotic joust to get a new baseball stadium built where many thought it really belonged, in the heart of the city's Over-the-Rhine, north of the riverfront in a neighborhood where an entertainment district was blossoming spontaneously—not back on the sterile, freeway-fenced riverfront where it ended up. On a parking lot called Broadway Commons, Tarbell painted an entire diamond, complete with base paths and dugouts. Later, after Tarbell's helium balloons had deflated, Cincinnati's unofficial board of directors on the Cincinnati Business Committee shook their heads and dismissed his two-dimensional parking-lot stadium like something born from a clinically manic imagination that sees grandiose golden-harp visions in a handful of dry beans. The crusade did not get "Baseball on Broadway," but it got Tarbell on City Council.

On April 9, 2001, Jim Tarbell was just one more shell-shocked council member, trying to bring the meeting to order like a man trying to stop a furniture-smashing bar brawl by tinking a spoon against a crystal wine goblet. Nobody listened.

Because of all that followed—three days of rioting that crippled a great city, the worst riots in Cincinnati since the 1960s and the worst race riots in America since the Rodney King riots in Los Angeles ten years earlier—because of all that, the debacle at City Hall on April 9, 2001, was almost overlooked and forgotten, like a fatal bullet carelessly swept up in broken glass at a crime scene.

There was never an investigation. Nobody formed a blue-ribbon panel to find out how things could go so wrong. There was no task force appointed to ask how a mob seized control of City Hall in one of the largest cities in America. There was no mayor's commission assigned to tell the public how Cincinnati's elected leaders could be held in a suffocating headlock for nearly four hours while City Hall's own public access TV and council's own microphones were used to broadcast calls for violence and threats that incited a race riot.

There was never even any discussion to find out why the Cincinnati riots of 2001 began in—of all the bizarre, ironic places—the Law and Public Safety Committee.

But that meeting on April 9 was one of the great institutional failures that contributed to beatings, looting, intimidation, threats, chaos, a crime wave, record murders, an infestation of drug gangs, a police slowdown, boycotts, lawsuits, federal monitors, a Department of Justice investigation and the long, steady decline of Cincinnati's law and public safety.

What began that afternoon at City Hall was like the first broken tree limb falling on a power line, that shorts out a transformer and begins the cascade of blown fuses, fried relays and grid failures that ripple outward like shock waves until an entire region is blacked out for days. City Council was just the first institution to fail. Its fall went almost unnoticed because it was so quickly followed by other toppled dominoes: the police, the media, the courts, business leaders, civil rights leaders, churches, politicians. They Humpty-Dumptied for days, months and even years after April 9, 2001. And all the king's horses and all the king's men could not put the pieces together again.

So that meeting is worth another look.

÷ ÷ ÷

John Cranley, one of the youngest and least experienced council members, was thrust in the role of chairman of the meeting, appointed by the mayor as a reward for Cranley's role as a rising young star in the Democratic Party and a loyal, dependable vote for the mayor's proposals. A likeable, sunny and earnest lawyer, Cranley was a walking contradiction—a West Side Democrat, raised in the traditionally Republican, family-values neighborhood of working-class Price Hill, but educated at the citadel of liberal culture, Harvard Law School and Harvard Divinity School.

In his first campaign, he was the sacrificial lamb in a steep uphill race against a popular West Sider incumbent Republican Congressman Steve Chabot—and Cranley surprised Cincinnati by getting 44 percent of the vote. That later vaulted him into an appointed seat on City Council— where he was dragged into the political corn picker by an accident of circumstance, as chairman of the Law and Public Safety Committee.

Fate, friendship and politics could not have made a worse choice, other council members said later.

There were more seasoned council members available. Phil Heimlich or Pat DeWine both had more experience. It's not much of a reach to assume that either one might have headed off the disaster that Cranley allowed or unintentionally encouraged with the uncertain weakness he tried to hide behind a frozen smile. But Heimlich and DeWine each had a disqualifying problem—they were Republicans, and City Council was dominated by Democrats. So the Republicans were passed over by Luken in favor of a guy whom press and politicians often compared to Jerry Mathers on "Leave it to Beaver"—John Cranley.

Most of the time, sending a rookie in as committee chairman was harmless. On April 9, it was about as harmless as putting a Mousketeer in charge of a maximum-security cellblock.

Cranley began the meeting about 1 p.m. with a promise to dispense with all of the regular business and a sincere call to prayer.

"We have some difficult times in front of us now," Cranley said, referring to the police shooting of an unarmed black suspect in a dark alley two nights before. Swallowing hard, he wiped his brow and his eyes darted around the room like a guy dragged in front of an angry Diversity Committee to stand trial for "hate speech." Cranley was broadcasting his nervousness while he asked for calm.

"And I ask that everyone should pray we get through this."

Most of the crowd was not listening.

Most were busy watching a man who wore a garish yellow-and-black African robe and matching pillbox hat as he paraded back and forth, directly in front of the crescent of council tables, waving a sign the size of a car door: "Stop Killing Us or Else" it said in scrawled red spray paint, the words unevenly spaced and crowded so the letters jammed up and fell over the edge to the next line.

Council members knew trouble was coming that day. But they had instructed the Cincinnati Police they didn't want any officers in the room. "We were told no uniformed cops would be allowed," said a SWAT commander later. "They said it might upset the crowd."

For months, going back to the previous Democratic Mayor Roxanne Qualls, Council meetings had been slipping out of control. Qualls, a former house painter and remodeler who got into politics as an environmental activist, had her own dust-ups with council members at meetings that became increasingly strident and hostile. Cincinnati's famous manners were being worn through at the elbows. And soon the crowds joined in to tear the meetings apart at the seams.

Each week, the shouts, protests, interruptions and outbursts would gradually escalate. For the most part, council members and the mayor ignored them, as if the grunts and shouts were too undignified to deserve notice. But the "We don't see anything" act didn't fool anyone. As the council members looked the other way and pretended not to notice, the loudest black protesters shouted about "Niggernati" and "white devils" and lobbed high-octane accusations of racism against anyone who disagreed, starting with the Cincinnati Police.

Citizens who came to Council meetings or stumbled on them on Public Access cable TV watched in disbelief and wondered in letters to the editor how the circus looked to outsiders. "Can you imagine if someone was coming to town, thinking of bringing a business to Cincinnati, and they see this on their hotel TV?" they asked. How can I take my children or students to a council meeting with this going on?" they wondered.

A few columns and tepid editorials were written to urge more civility. By the time the editorials were massaged and filtered for political correctness, they usually blamed council members as much as the yahoos in the audience—just to be evenhanded. Most editors and reporters just threw a free-speech blanket over it, mumbled something about tolerance and diversity, and tucked the edges down tight to hide the smell of fermenting anger. The yahoos were black. And most opinion leaders of Cincinnati lacked the backbone to call them out and risk being labeled as racists.

To the protesters, who apparently had their afternoons free to attend meetings every week, it was all a great game—their own reality TV show.

"I heard you called me a racist," General Kabaka Oba told a columnist after being criticized for his rants about the white devils" and the "Jewnited Snakes of America."

"Next time you call me a racist, I want it on Page One," said the bus driver and self-promoted leader of "The Black Fist," an army that had no majors, sergeants, corporals, privates or even any Kentucky Colonels which are as common as KFC franchises.

In July of 2000, Mayor Charlie Luken had to ask deputies to remove Jimmy Hardy, who protested under the name of Abdul Muhammad Ali, always wearing a red and black leather cap displaying the ironic word "UNITY." Hardy/Ali was charged with disorderly conduct for repeatedly interrupting meetings with grunts, shouts and outbursts. At one meeting, he called Luken a "punk faggot."

When Hardy went to court, he subpoenaed the entire council, and won acquittal when Councilman Charles Winburn testified that the shouting by Muhammad Ali was really no problem. Hardy's winning lawyer was the "Law Dog," Ken Lawson.

After that, trying to maintain order during public comments or any-time during meetings was laughable. The class clown had challenged the school principal—and won.

"There was an anti-police attitude among politicians," Police Chief Tom Streicher said, looking back. "The antics in council, widely broad-cast, showed total disregard of any respect for authority. I think that fueled the riots more than anything."

÷ ÷ ÷

On April 9, council members stuttered and stammered to delay the loom-ing confrontation like school kids taking the long way home to avoid a bully. They glanced with wide eyes to see the room filled far past capacity. They knew something was really out of control this time.

Soon there were two guys picketing between the crowd and the coun-cil members, waving big signs. Soon the boos were cascading and drown-ing out council members as they tried to stick to their script. The man in yellow, with the car-door-sized sign, walked right into the area that usual-ly divides council from the audience, and Cranley didn't ask him to move or call for security. He blinked, swallowed and just kept stammering, "Can I . . . Can I . . . Can I have . . . Can I have . . . Can I have order please?"

Nobody listened.

"I don't know what to do," he said, turning to the other council mem-bers.

"Get a gavel," someone suggested in a voice that was hanging by fin-gernails on the cliff-edge of panic.

Tarbell and Heimlich both separately urged Cranley to shut down the meeting. "He said, 'I can't, they would kill me,'" Heimlich recalled later. "I think he meant it politically."

Sandy Sherman, Council Clerk for years, pointed at the man in yel-low and told Cranley, "That man needs to take a seat." But nobody on council did anything about it.

The protesters kept circling closer like hammerheads closing in on a struggling swimmer. There was blood in the water, and everyone could smell it.

William Kirkland, a regular protester who tormented council as if every meeting was junior-high social studies with a nervous substitute teacher, began shouting and never stopped. "We may want to recess,"

Tarbell tersely told Cranley.

"Let's adjourn for 20 minutes," Cranley agreed, nodding as if he had just figured out the right answer. It *was* the right answer, Tarbell, cops and other council members all said later. It was the smart thing to do. Just walk out. Demonstrate that council would not tolerate such shouting and abuse. Show the mob who was in control. Let them all know they would not be allowed to hijack a city meeting. They could have the empty room—but they would not get to take council hostage. It was exactly the right thing to do.

But then Cranley changed his mind.

"If we don't have order, we're going to recess," he announced—triggering a deafening crescendo of boos, screaming and insults. "I can't deal with this," he mumbled, thinking he was off the microphone. At one point he tried to leave and was roughed up and shaken by the crowd. He finally began banging his gavel like he was hammering plywood over windows in the teeth of a hurricane. Soon even his frantic rapping was lost in the crashing sea of noise.

One man in the crowd jumped up on a polished wooden conference table where the city solicitor was supposed to be seated. The microphones went out, fried by the overload of noise. Then they blared back on and Cranley announced that he would give the floor to . . . one of the loudest shouters, William Kirkland.

Even Kirkland could not be heard, though, and after a few stumbling attempts, he gave up and the waves of chaos came crashing back.

At that moment council member Alicia Reece arrived in a flurry, grabbed a microphone and announced that even though she was not a member of the Law and Public Safety Committee, she was there because, "What we're seeing here today is the frustration in our city."

The 20-something former Miss Grambling was convinced she was on track to be the next mayor. She had finished near the top in the most recent council elections, and was assured by her supporters that her star was destined to keep rising. Her father, Steve Reece, was Jesse Jackson's best friend in Cincinnati, and was a political player from his Integrity Hall base in Bond Hill.

Later, even a few of her Democratic Party allies on council acknowledged that Reece had not accomplished much. Her critics pointed out that she was too quick to blame others and resort to playing the race card as an answer for every setback or defeated motion.

Among council members, she was not popular. Privately, council members would shake their heads and say, "Alicia is all about Alicia."

But today, she was on her game, enjoying the moment, more than happy to use the crowd the way she often did, wading in just deep enough to feel the strong undertow, then running to get ahead of the wave and ride it wherever it crashed. She flashed a big smile like her team was winning.

"Every member of this council from the mayor down needs to hear this," scolded Reece.

Some who were at the meeting claimed they heard her say, "I'm lovin' it." If she did, it did not show up on a tape of the meeting. But the encouragement she gave to the mob and her angry, indignant mockery of city officials helped to blow out a few more circuit breakers between order and violence. It certainly looked like she was "lovin' it."

Cranley seemed relieved to let Reece take over. Although several members of the Law and Public Safety Committee had been asking for a chance to speak, he turned the floor over to Reece. He seemed almost grateful that Reece took the time out of her busy day to stop by and run his meeting.

But Reece quickly lost her tenuous grip and control slipped away again. When Ken "Law Dog" Lawson arrived at the witness table in front of the council members, all eyes turned to watch the flamboyant, growling street-fighter who had repeatedly sued City Hall and the Cincinnati Police, and often won.

Lawson, who adopted the Law Dog title along with pit bull mascots, was on the attack.

He took a seat at a table facing council, jammed in by the crowd, flanked by a man in black with a black beret and shades, who was doing a good impression of an Eldridge Cleaver on the cover of "Soul on Ice."

In the middle of it all, Lawson managed to look cool and comfortable, not fazed at all. He was at ease, in charge.

Sitting next to Lawson were the family of police-shooting victim Timothy Thomas: his girlfriend, sister and grieving mother, Angela Leisure.

Cranley made one last desperate attempt. This time, he gave the floor to Lawson. Then he said, "To have this meeting survive, if people talk out of order, they're going to be removed."

He was hooted down with laughter and insults. Having already abandoned the idea of adjourning the meeting and removing the council members, Cranley threatened the impossible—"removing" a crowd that outnumbered council members and city officials by at least 20 to one, with no uniformed cops in sight.

As another wave of boos and shouts immediately drowned out Cranley and his threat to have people removed, Councilman Paul Booth leaned over and advised Cranley, "Let it go." He did. The crowd suddenly went quiet as Lawson began speaking in a quiet, normal voice about "all the brothers who have been shot and choked to death by the police."

"There's a cover-up going on," Lawson accused—and the shouting rage was unleashed again, dialed up another notch.

"If you are a black male, you will run from the cops," shouted Leisure. And the noise went up another decibel.

Now the crowd had pushed, elbowed and shoved its way in directly behind council members' seats, and the politicians were surrounded.

Lawson took control of the microphones. He demanded to know what happened to Thomas. The crowd simmered to a low rumble, waiting for an answer, as random shouts and stray screams punctuated the pause.

Tarbell replied by reading the official report: Thomas saw an officer who was after him because he was wanted on 14 warrants, he read. Thomas ran east on 13th, south on Jackson, and west on 12th. He jumped a fence, ran across a parking lot with police in pursuit, climbed another fence and came out a narrow alley on Republic just as Officer Stephen Roach arrived, responding in his cruiser to calls for help with pursuit of a suspect wanted on warrants. Roach ran down an alley to intercept Thomas, and as the fleeing suspect came around a corner, Roach shot him.

As he tried to read on, Tarbell was shouted down again and Cranley called on Lawson, who in turn yelled, "Why did you shoot him?" It hit the crowd like kerosene on a bonfire.

Tarbell looked stricken, as if Lawson had accused *him* of shooting Thomas.

As the storm swept over council members, Cincinnati Mayor Charlie Luken arrived and took a seat two chairs down from Cranley.

The former congressman and TV anchor was the son of Congressman Tom Luken, and the latest successful politician in the Luken family, which had a long tradition of leadership in the Democratic Party.

But Mayor Luken did nothing to take control of the meeting from

Cranley, who was flailing like a drowning man. And he did nothing to throw a rescue line to City Manager John Shirey, either, who Reece summoned a few minutes later to face the crowd. Luken sat there in his shirt sleeves with his chin cradled in his hands like a student in class, looking as inconspicuous as a council aide or city staffer. After an hour, he quietly got up and went back to his office, where the meltdown of Cincinnati was showing live on TV.

"In retrospect, we should have just adjourned the meeting," he said later. "We were trying to be respectful, while people were jousting around us, pushing on the back of my chair. We were trying very hard to be sympathetic."

Luken said he decided there was nothing he could do. "I personally think too much emphasis has been put on that meeting as the origin of the riots," he said. "It was not the first meeting that got out of hand."

As Luken left, Lawson switched gears and said that his next "only question" was to know why Leisure was never notified about her son's death by the police. Shirey said he was told she had been notified by Lieutenant Colonel Ron Twitty.

"Where's Twitty?" people in the crowd began shouting in unison.

Cranley again turned the meeting over to the crowd. "Please listen to Mr. Lawson," he pleaded into his microphone.

Next, the crowd demanded Safety Director Kent Ryan. "I hope he's not hiding back there somewhere," Reece mocked.

City Manager John Shirey looked nervous. A transplant from Long Beach, California, where he was an assistant city manager, Shirey graduated from Purdue University with a degree in industrial engineering before earning a master's degree in public administration at the University of Southern California. He was also a track and field referee who had officiated at the 1996 Olympics—but no striped shirt or whistle could help him now. He looked over his shoulder for an exit. Too late. The man in yellow was swinging his sign right in the faces of council members, so they had to flinch and dodge to avoid getting bumped.

A woman in a black dress began shouting and fanning herself furiously with a scrap of paper, screaming at the top of her lungs in a voice like broken glass, parroting whatever Lawson demanded—when she made sense at all.

It was painfully clear—council had lost the last shred of its authority.

There was not even any pretense that council members were in control. They were now only the most reasonable part of an insane mob, doing its bidding, rephrasing the ridiculous screamed demands in almost rational language, summoning whomever the crowd demanded, struggling like a mugger's victim to comply with the most absurd requests and offer polite, logical answers to bizarre insults and impossible demands. The guillotine-happy Jacobins in the French Revolution would have felt right at home as they listened to the mob yell for the another city department head.

If the crowd had demanded the immediate lynching of Officer Roach, council members probably would have at least pledged to appoint a blue-ribbon committee to shop for the rope.

Finally, Police Chief Thomas Streicher arrived in a light olive civilian jacket and tie, so at first he was hard to spot. He did not announce his presence. That was done for him by a crescendo of boos signaling that the police chief had entered the eye of the storm. As the pandemonium temporarily subsided, Lawson raised his arms to demand quiet and repeated his litany of "just one question" demands. He wanted to know what happened, why the cop shot Thomas, what was Roach's explanation.

Streicher patiently explained that he had already met with Hamilton County Prosecutor Mike Allen, and all of the investigative files had been subpoenaed by a grand jury. "That takes it out of the hands of the police division," he said.

Lawson threw his head on the table in histrionic disgust, but he should have known as an experienced criminal defense lawyer that the specific crime scene details he was demanding could only be delivered at the risk of jeopardizing the investigation and possible prosecution.

Streicher continued to explain, in the "just the facts" voice of a polite cop at a traffic stop, that releasing evidence publicly could undermine a criminal investigation and prevent possible prosecution of Roach. But then the chief did his best to give Lawson exactly the answers he had been demanding.

"I can simply say to you," he said, "that Officer Roach reacted to what he perceived as a threat from the other person."

There it was. All the hours of screaming to find out what anyone could have learned from the morning newspaper. Roach said he fired the shot because he thought Thomas was reaching for a gun.

It was the answer Lawson had demanded. But it was not the one the crowd wanted. So they ignored it as if Streicher had flatly refused to say anything.

"We want action," they began to chant in unison, as young men strutted and danced on tables and sat down to spin back and forth in empty council seats. A news photo shows an angry, goateed black man in a Guess Jeans T-shirt, leaning over Streicher, pounding the table, pointing his finger, eyes popping, threatening the Cincinnati Police chief.

It's an image that Cincinnati cops never forgot. It symbolized in one snapshot the frustration and anger they felt, trying to do their best in a difficult situation, while being insulted and threatened.

The screaming woman in the black dress kept hopping like her feet were on fire, her face twisted in rage. Lawson kept making demands. Council members kept looking for a safe way out. Cranley suddenly announced, "The Rev. Damon Lynch wants to speak."

A hush fell over the crowd again. Here was the city's New and Improved Civil Rights Leader, the boss of the Black United Front and its boycott of Cincinnati, the pastor of New Prospect Baptist Church, a well-educated middle-class son of an almost legendary local civil rights leader and preacher, the Rev. Damon Lynch Jr.

Cranley looked as relieved as a wagon-train settler down to his last bullet who has just seen the cavalry riding to the rescue.

Damon Lynch III stood next to Lawson in an untucked white BUF T-shirt, grabbed a microphone and announced:

"Nobody leaves these chambers until we get the answer. Members of the Black United Front are standing at the doors, because nobody leaves until we get an answer."

Tarbell was shocked. A violent threat from a reverend. In the time it took for the words to sink in, the protests crossed yet another invisible line and began to stagger over the edge into race riots.

Two hours and 50 minutes into the meeting it was official: Council was now held hostage in its own City Hall. All hell broke loose. "Long hot summer," the crowd yelled, dropping the "F"-bomb like a hailstorm. "We're gonna tear this city up."

"I don't know what more we can tell you," Shirey said plaintively. He was ignored.

Lieutenant Colonel Ron Twitty showed up to "testify," but now the crowd was listening only for entertainment.

"I don't know what I'm supposed to be responding to," Twitty began, confused. He tried to explain how he had struggled to contact Leisure to tell her about her son, but she had moved and left no address. He finally tracked her down through her daughter and found her at the hospital. But as he tried to explain, Leisure was not at the table with Lawson anymore.

Twitty tried to explain how the investigation would be torn wide open if all the details were thrown to the mob. "I know Mr. Lawson knows this," he said.

And at that, the Law Dog howled. "You run that on somebody else," he shouted. "Don't you ever tell me what I know."

"That's when I showed my temper," Lawson said later. "It was almost as if someone told him, 'These are your people, get 'em under control.' When I saw him being used like that, and he knew he was being used, that made me angry."

But Twitty was right. Lawson was one of the top defense lawyers in town. And any attorney would know that what Twitty, Streicher, Shirey and Tarbell said was true. They had done all they could to answer Lawson's questions without compromising the case.

By then it was all over but the shouting. And the broken glass. And the rock throwing, the fires, looting, beatings and race riots.

Leisure returned to the table and called Twitty "a habitual liar." Cranley begged Lawson for permission to speak. Reece yelled, "Hey, Kenny," hoping to catch the attention of the only person who seemed to have any control of the mob. Lawson ignored her and continued to demand answers. Lynch reminded the council members they were trapped.

Meanwhile, Tarbell announced, "LADIES AND GENTLEMEN . . . LADIES AND GENTLEMEN . . . LADIES AND GENTLEMEN . . . LADIES AND GENTLEMEN . . . LADIES AND GENTLEMEN . . . LADIES AND GENTLEMEN . . . LADIES AND GENTLEMEN . . ."

Finally, the knocking paid off. The door opened a crack and most began to listen.

"I'm going to tell you what the officers told me," Tarbell said in the narrow gap between shouts.

He tried to explain that the cop thought his life was in danger, that the alley where the shooting occurred is a war zone where guns are as common as crack pipes. "I'm trying to give you information that's on the street," he said. "For us to stay here any longer and yell and scream at one another when most of us were not there is not helping anyone."

Lynch took a spot in front of the crowd and delivered a long manifesto, but the crowd was already beginning to tune out and filter out, moving with one mind back into the streets. They had humiliated the top elected leaders and government officials of the city. They had heard Lawson and Lynch threaten city council members and they saw that nothing was done to stop them.

Just shouting "We want action" was no longer enough. They wanted the real thing. And as they spilled out the doors like a chemical reaction gone wrong in the Frankenstein's castle of local government, they were joined by bigger crowds waiting outside, drawn to City Hall by the City Cable broadcast of disorder and threats at the Law and Public Safety meeting.

The worst meeting in the history of City Hall was finally over. The worst for Cincinnati was just about to begin.

Flanked by Ohio State Highway Patrol
and Cincinnati Police commanders,
Mayor Charlie Luken, Police Chief Thomas
Streicher and City Manager John Shirey
(left to right) held a press conference.
Luken called in 75 state troopers and
announced a curfew on April 12.

CHAPTER 3

LEADERLESS IN CINCINNATI

With cone-capped turrets of purple-brown brick, arched cathedral windows and roofs so steep they would give acrophobia to a sparrow, Cincinnati City Hall is a gothic-looking old haunted house of government. The architecture is Romanesque, but more recognizable these days as a distant cousin of Dr. Frankenstein's castle.

After the council meeting meltdown, it looked like the villagers had already been there with pitchforks and torches, and the awakened monster was now on the loose.

On their way out of the Law and Public Safety Committee hearing, the mob had smashed windows—and then returned again later to smash more. A local lawyer and City Hall regular, Robert Manley, said he investigated and found that the contractor who replaced the windows claimed more than 200 were broken. City workers confirmed that, Manley said. But City Manager John Shirey insisted it was only a dozen or so.

Shirey still keeps a cartoon about it in his California office. The drawing by *The Cincinnati Enquirer's* cartoonist Jim Borgman has council members standing in front of the broken windows at City Hall—blaming Shirey.

City managers are like the Secret Service of politics—their job is to be constantly ready and willing to take a bullet for their politicians' blunders. But for Shirey, most of the wounds came from being shot in the back by council members as they formed a circular firing squad each week and put Shirey in the middle.

Near the end of his time at City Hall, Shirey became known around the *Enquirer* newsroom as "Eeyore," after the despondent donkey in Winnie the Pooh. In Shirley's world, it was always raining and the forecast every day was mostly gloomy.

But while buildings burned and stores were being looted that week in April, he was still the city manager in one of America's historic great cities. In those hours of Cincinnati's greatest crisis, with all of his training and experience in eight years of running City Hall on the line, he said he was called on to—sit down and shut up.

Stunned and shaken by the pandemonium that had erupted in City Hall that afternoon, Shirey, Police Chief Thomas Streicher, Safety Director Kent Ryan and other key city officials huddled in Shirey's first-floor office to respond to the growing violence on that first day of the riots.

"Kent was sitting immediately to my left at my large conference table," Shirey recalled. "As the meeting progressed, it was clear to everyone that something was wrong with Kent. He was sweating profusely and uncomfortable. He was coherent, though, and said he was OK. After the meeting, Kent and the chief left together. I learned later in the evening that the chief had taken Kent to University Hospital and he had been admitted. I don't remember what the final diagnosis was."

Reports the next day said Ryan had suffered a heart attack. As Streicher was taking Ryan to Ryan's home and waiting for an ambulance there, the window-smashing mob left City Hall and headed for police headquarters, where Assistant Chief Ron Twitty was left in charge—and wound up handing a bullhorn to rock-throwing rioters.

"He was in stroke territory," Streicher said of Ryan. "Very white, sweating."

"Kent never returned to his post as safety director," Shirey said. "I did not have his service the rest of that incident. I think it was the next day that I made Streicher acting safety director, which to me was the obvious choice. I learned some time later that various people were critical of my decision to make Streicher the acting director. Another example of how I couldn't win no matter what I did."

Streicher remembers something quite different during the emergency meeting in Shirey's office.

"He pointed to me and said, 'What do you want me to do? I can't fire him. If I could fire him, I would do it right now and this thing would be over.'"

Shirey was willing to throw him to the sharks for a quick political solution, Streicher said. After the others left, Streicher confronted Shirey. "He denied it. I was sitting right there and heard him and he denied it."

÷÷÷

A few years earlier, that crisis-management meeting in Shirey's office might have been quite different. Even in the 90s, Cincinnati still had a strong tradition of civic involvement and support from local business leaders. It was the "Cincinnatus" tradition, named after the Roman soldier and general who left his farm and came out of retirement to save Rome—then refused to become emperor and went back to his fields.

In the early 1990s, the Cincinnati Business Committee, composed of two dozen top business leaders representing the Fortune 500 corporations that gave the city its "Blue Chip City" nickname, still made most of the big decisions for the city. They created the Smale Commission to study and improve the city's aging streets and infrastructure, named after John Smale, Chairman of Proctor & Gamble and then General Motors. They created the Buenger Commission to save the decaying, waste-riddled public schools, named after Clem Buenger, chairman of the city's biggest local bank with the mathematically impossible merged name, Fifth-Third. As late as the mid-90s, the CBC had its executive director make weekly contacts with the city manager to offer directions and very firm suggestions that were seldom refused, given the enormous financial and political clout of CBC donors who funded campaigns for council and much of the civic philanthropy in town.

To outsiders, that corporate shadow government looked like a relic, a throwback to the old "smoke-filled rooms" where public decisions were made in private board rooms, without the nuisance of public interference and participation. Sure enough, some of the CBC decisions were too cozy—no-bid contracts that channeled public money to local businesses, for example. To critics, it was a "corpocracy"—government by and for corporations.

By the end of the 1990s, that was also becoming the public perception, and a slate of CBC government reform proposals were rejected by voters.

Only later, after Cincinnati had cast off the shackles of corpocracy, did the city finally realize how many positive things the CBC had done. By then, it was too late. Too many family-owned businesses had been merged or bought, handed over to ladder-climbing outsiders with MBAs, who had no intention of making Cincinnati their permanent home. They just wanted to fill in their resumes and move on to Dallas, Atlanta, New York or Los Angeles. By then, the Cincinnatus tradition was as stiff as the bronzed statue of the Roman hero on the riverfront.

But Cincinnati faced another problem. The political muscle at City Hall had atrophied from years of leaning on the crutch of business leadership. Forced to stand up and walk on its own, the council and mayor were wobbly, uncertain and slow at a critical time of crisis that called for strong, sure and decisive leadership.

Even ten years earlier, it would be impossible to imagine the meeting in Shirey's office without one or two CBC business leaders in the room to offer wise counsel and crisis-calming support.

"Where were they when we needed them most?" Councilman Jim Tarbell wonders.

To illustrate, he tells the story of the time he tried to seek advice and support from the CBC for his crusade to get the new Reds baseball stadium built on Broadway Commons. Tarbell met with the CBC President at the time, Jim Zimmerman, chairman of Cincinnati-based Federated Department Stores. He said Zimmerman told him, "You might be right, but I just don't know—I'm not even here anymore."

The CBC of the past was the true Cincinnatus spirit—the local men whose families had built the giant corporations that made Cincinnati wealthy and stable. They stepped in to help the city with purely volunteer effort, expertise and enormous financial resources.

If some of those business leaders had been in the room in the critical meetings during the first few days, perhaps the city might have handled things differently. Perhaps their public relations skills and experience would have spared Cincinnati the unfair national reputation as a racist city where violent rogue cops shoot down young black men in the streets.

Looking back, Shirey said the first mistake was the Law and Public Safety meeting.

"It is easy to second-guess certain council members' decision to hold the meeting," he said. "In their defense, they thought not having the meeting would only cause more unrest on the street. Their reasoning was 'Let people vent here in council chambers and not act out on the streets.' The mistake in having the meeting was not having a game plan for the meeting. It would have been better to confer with the safety director, the police chief and me beforehand. That, of course, never happened. The three of us should never have been put in the position we were in during that meeting. We had had a serious shooting incident. The investigation was underway, and we were not sure all of our officers were telling the truth. There was a possibility that criminal charges could be brought against one or more officers. Anything we said during the public meeting could have jeopardized the investigation and/or the criminal charges. We explained the situation as well as we could at the meeting, but as you saw, it was not good enough to satisfy the crowd and some members of council. Imagine how much we would have been criticized later if we said something to jeopardize the investigation or a criminal charge."

The other mistake occurred after that meeting, in an emergency conference with Mayor Charlie Luken, Shirey said.

"As far as the issue of 'control' was concerned, what I remember vividly was a meeting in my office that included the mayor, a few council members, and some city staff—perhaps the chief—wherein the mayor announced without discussion that he would be the only spokesman for the city and that he would handle the press. No one challenged him, including myself. Normally, spokesperson chores during a serious incident would be split between the city manager and the mayor.

"When the events of that week were over, I concluded that his decision and my decision were poor ones. Since he was the visible face of the city in the press, he had to take ownership of the unrest, which was not good for him. Since I was not visible, some people concluded that I was missing in action and not doing my job, which was not good for me. It would have been better if we had worked together."

That confusion did mortal damage to Cincinnati. Within hours, Luken went on CNN and announced: "There's a great deal of frustration within the community, which is understandable. We've had way too many deaths in our community at the hands of Cincinnati police. I'm not asking anyone not to be frustrated, but to just realize in the short-term someone could get hurt."

The remarks were devastating. They seemed to ratify the worst accusations against the city and the police. To the national press, Luken's comments were used to confirm that even the mayor believed the worst exaggerations by the protest and boycott leader the Rev. Damon Lynch III and his Black United Front.

By blaming the police first, Luken poisoned his relationship with Cincinnati cops during the riots and for years afterward, aggravating City Hall attacks on the cops that eventually led to a devastating police slow-down that ushered in Cincinnati's worst crime wave in generations. His remarks kicked off a parade of uninformed attacks on Cincinnati, especially in the media. And they set the tone of coverage nationally, casting Cincinnati in the role of Racist City, USA and giving oxygen to what had been a dying boycott.

Citizens who knew better and supported the police were outraged and demoralized by Luken's comment. What he seemed to say is that it was OK to tear up a city in "frustration," because the rioters were expressing justified anger, not incoherent violence and reckless thuggery.

As it turns out, Luken was all wrong. There were not "way too many deaths" at the hands of police. Even including an atypical spike in fatal police shootings, Cincinnati's rate was far below the rates in similar cities. And nearly all of the shootings were indisputably justified. Even the ones that were described as "troubling" in newspaper reports and editorials involved suspects who violently resisted arrest.

But by the time CNN had broadcast Luken's remarks to the world, it was too late. To the news-watching nation, Cincinnati's young black men were all Rodney King, and Cincinnati police were beating them down with flailing batons.

During the critical first hours of the riots, when fast, decisive application of overwhelming force can make all the difference to protect life and property and restore sanity and public safety, Cincinnati was leaderless and confused. When political leaders should have backed up the police, they instead undermined them and threatened to fire the chief in the middle of a crisis. The police still did their jobs—heroically in many cases—but they went into the streets, risking their lives, knowing that the political leaders would cut and run at the first sign of trouble. Sure enough, as soon as a fragile peace was restored, the politicians and bureaucrats began blaming the cops again.

Less than a month after the riots, John Shirey was forced to resign by city council, for being inept and failing to show leadership during the riots—a performance evaluation that could have been written about nearly everyone at City Hall.

Michael Howard grew up on the rough streets of the West End and Over-the-Rhine. He now runs a shelter for ex-convicts called Justice Watch on Garden Street in the West End.

CHAPTER 4

"LIKE ESCAPE FROM NEW YORK"

The Erie Canal ran like a manmade river through the north end of downtown Cincinnati until it was drained, filled with dirt and paved with cobblestones in 1928. The German immigrants who built Cincinnati and crowded the tenements, shops and outdoor beer gardens north of the canal named the muddy ditch "the little Rhine." When they went home at night after working in the tanneries, soap factories, pork-packing plants and breweries, they crossed bridges over the canal and returned to their neighborhood of tall red-brick apartments like cliff dwellings, with unpainted wooden stairs and banners of laundry strung from upper windows. Soon the neighborhood north of the canal became known as "Over-the-Rhine."

In 1850, 43,000 people lived in less than one square mile in Over-the-Rhine, and 75 percent were German immigrants. By 1927, the year before the stagnant, unhealthy Erie Canal had to be drained, most of the 17 breweries in the neighborhood had been closed by Prohibition.

By 1990, the population had shrunk to less than 10,000 and was now 71 percent black—but more poor than ever. By 2005, it had dwindled to about 7,500.

An illustration by Norman Rockwell of a WWII soldier coming home to the crowded brick canyons of inner-city apartments could have been painted in Over-the-Rhine. Even today, along crumbling, littered streets lit by gaudy neon, where dope boys slouch on corners in drooping inmate jeans, waiting for SUVs of suburban white kids to buy weed and rock, you can still spot German signs in peeling, faded paint that cling to old brick walls, announcing "Apotheker" drug stores and "Biergartens."

In the 1970s, a hippie on the run from his square suburban middle-class past moved into and seized old buildings in Over-the-Rhine in the name of "social justice." Buddy Gray and his Restoc activist group turned one old hulk into a homeless shelter, and city officials backed down and let him stay. The decline of Over-the-Rhine accelerated like coal rolling down a chute. Soon the old neighborhood that visiting architects said was like a time capsule of untouched, preserved historic housing, became a wildlife refuge for social workers and their endless stream of clients. Over-the-Rhine became the city's attic, to store halfway houses, soup kitchens, counseling centers, group homes for the mentally ill and parolees, food banks, church missions and almost anything nobody else wanted.

On April 10, 2001, the second day of the riots, the old Erie Canal, now a wide, grass-divided boulevard named Central Parkway, became another kind of German landmark: it was the unofficial Berlin Wall that separated most of the looting, arson and beatings in Over-the-Rhine from the office workers, stores, restaurants and corporate skyscrapers in the downtown business district to the south.

Late that night, Cincinnati Police Captain Paul Humphries was driving the wrong way south on Elm Street in Over-the-Rhine, past Findlay Market, one of the oldest outdoor farm markets in the nation. It was dark. The sky was lit by the red glow of fires and smudged with a layer of acrid smoke.

"I was swerving around all this stuff in the street," Humphries remembers. "There was a burning, tipped-over garbage can, and I went around that. And then there was a pile of burning clothes I had to go around. There was stuff in the street everywhere. Bottles were hitting the hood of my car. There were shots being fired, buildings on fire.

"I thought it looked like a scene from that movie, 'Escape from New York.' It was so strange."

The day had been a long, frightening hell of looting, beatings and arson in Over-the-Rhine.

"Anyone can work a 12-hour shift," Humphries recalls. "But this was 12 hours of constantly fighting fires, keeping people from breaking into places, nonstop from one to the next, wondering if you're going to be shot, bullets flying everywhere."

Throughout the day, the cops used rubber bullets and beanbag shotguns that fire a non-lethal bag of pellets to stop looters. They fired canisters of "clear out" pepper sprays. They ducked flying rocks and bottles, and marched down streets with their elbows locked, banging their clear shields with batons.

They followed crowds of young thugs and rioters as they went wild down streets, carrying signs, wearing bandana masks like Wild West train robbers, breaking windows, setting stores on fire, stealing shoes, clothing and TVs while police cruisers crept along behind them like some kind of bizarre escort for a parade of crime and insanity.

On WDBZ, the new AM station that laid claim on being the new voice of black Cincinnati, talk show hosts and callers gave on-air reports from the midst of the rioting, describing the scene in vivid detail as looters stepped through gaping holes in shattered store windows, emerging with armloads of designer warm-up suits and bling.

While the city officials met with the Rev. Damon Lynch III to discuss his demands for social justice, while the media painted a picture of sanitized and justified "racial unrest" that had finally exploded after years of white oppression, the young teens and 20-something men and women who were smashing plate-glass windows and torching stores laughed, drank beer and posed on top of cars, mugging and striking body-builder poses for the news photographers. Unlucky white drivers who got stuck in blocked intersections were stoned with bricks or dragged from their cars and nearly "unrested" to death.

This was not "unrest." It was a race riot, an eruption of hate, crime and violence.

÷ ÷ ÷

Humphries admits the police could have done more to prevent it. "We all covered up and closed down," he said. During the critical hours after Timothy Thomas was shot and killed in an alley by Officer Stephen Roach as he ran from police, the police chief was out of town and nobody took charge to get in front of the story. Anger, rumors and paranoid accusations began to fill the vacuum. It was the same old story, repeated whenever a controversial violent arrest or police shooting happened. Time after time, the Cincinnati Police had a story of reasonable, justifiable police conduct to tell—but nobody stood up in front of the cameras, notebooks and microphones to tell it. That vacuum was usually filled by the angry, sharp-edged voice of Fraternal Order of Police President Keith Fangman. And most of the press seemed eager and willing to believe the Rodney-King worst about the cops.

Humphries, who got the nickname "Wonder Boy" by being one of the youngest captains in Cincinnati Police Division history, now believes things might have been different if someone had put the highest ranking black assistant chief, Ron Twitty, on TV and radio on Sunday, the day after the shooting, to explain as much as possible. But that was not even discussed. Instead, the rumors fermented until Monday afternoon, then exploded in screaming, hysterical chaos at the Law and Public Safety Committee in City Hall.

If he had been at that meeting, Humphries could have told Cincinnati all it needed to know about the shooting. When the fatal shots were fired at Timothy Thomas by Officer Stephen Roach, shortly after 2 a.m. on Saturday morning, Humphries was just a few blocks away, keeping an eye on the Main Street bars to decide if streets needed to be blocked off when the closing-time crowds spilled into the balmy spring streets.

When he got the radio call of "police in pursuit" of a suspect wanted on warrants, he knew exactly where to go. The alley where Thomas was shot was a favorite escape route of dopers and drug boys who worked Republic Street.

Humphries arrived one minute after the shooting. Two cops were already kneeling over the bleeding body of Thomas. "They were talking to him, telling him 'You're OK, hang on, an ambulance is on the way.' Steve was leaning against a wall there. He was short of breath and pale. He looked like he was gonna die too. I asked him if he was OK, and he said, 'My gun just went off.' I knew this was going to be bad. He just kept saying, 'Oh my God, oh my God, it just went off.'"

Later, after talking to lawyers, Roach insisted he shot Thomas because he thought Thomas was reaching for a weapon in his pants.

But an accidental shooting described by Humphries makes perfect sense to Cincinnati Police Training Institute Instructor Barry Andrews. To explain, he compared it to a cop who once reported taking fire from a suspect he thought was hiding in a locked bathroom stall. When backup arrived, they found the man dead, but unarmed. When someone checked the cop's revolver, they found he had fired the shot in a rush of adrenaline-fueled fear, and had not even realized it.

Andrews said the surest defense in Roach's situation was to claim it looked as if Thomas was reaching for a gun. With that story, it was what cops, courts and prosecutors call "a good shooting." An accidental discharge of a firearm might be a different story.

But as Roach stood there in the alley that night, rocking against the wall, nearly weeping in remorse, fear and confusion, a crowd began to gather. "This was different than any other shooting," Humphries recalls. "The crowd was angrier. There was that buzz going through the crowd. It was definitely more tense. You could tell this was not going to be good."

Three nights later he was driving his Ford Crown Victoria patrol car down Elm just a few blocks from the shooting, looking at a scene that could only be compared to a movie fantasy about a frightening future in which crime is so out of control the entire island of Manhattan is sealed off with razor-wire and abandoned as an unsupervised maximum-security prison.

The 'Escape From New York' comparison was not far off.

On April 10, the *Enquirer* reported that "police were investigating a report that an elderly man and woman were dragged from their Jeep and beaten with rocks by a roving gang at Walnut and Mercer streets in Over-the-Rhine."

The story never mentioned that the couple shared something in common with nearly every victim of riot violence. They were beaten because they were white.

Stories that even mentioned such attacks were rare. But cops noticed that the press had plenty of space to report grievances against the police. Stories about the second day included a man hit with rubber bullets who proudly displayed his bruises for a photo, and one of the most ironic quotes of the riots.

In a report on how "bystanders got caught up in the violence," new stories quoted a woman who said the Cincinnati police were overreacting. "I think it's crazy," she said. "I honestly do. It needs to stop. I just think they need to have better control over themselves."

Hundreds of black rioters were in the streets looting, setting fires and beating innocent white people—and it was the cops who "need to have better control of themselves."

TV cameras, reports on "Da Buzz" (WDBZ) that made the riots sound like a party and news stories that made it sound like the cops were causing the riots all made things worse, Humphries and many others cops believe.

"I think that was more of a contributing factor than us not saying anything. The news cameras there just encouraged the Black Panthers and gang members to act for the cameras. As soon as it would start getting dark, you'd see the masks coming out, and you knew bad things were going to happen."

Before they hit the streets, all the Cincinnati cops who were able and available to work gathered at Spinney Field, in the industrial Queensgate area west of downtown. The former practice camp for the Cincinnati Bengals NFL football team had been donated to the Cincinnati Police for offices and training.

Police Chief Tom Streicher and Lieutenant Colonel Richard Janke were there to send the cops out into the war zone.

Humphries says he will never forget the scene. "That first night at Spinney, as we were marshaling our forces, I was looking at the looks on the faces of the different kinds of cops there. Some of the veterans were ready. They had put their game faces on. Others were younger, new cops, wide-eyed, like, 'Oh my gosh.' Scared."

As they soldiered-up with bullet-proof vests, shields, weapons and helmets, listening to the chief's encouragement and morale-boosting support like a coach at halftime, just a few yards from a hash-marked Bengals practice field, some looked ready for the big game—and some looked like 8-year-olds being sent out to play in the NFL.

But they all went into those dark streets of flying bullets and burning trash. There was no escape from Cincinnati that night. Someone had to save the city.

They went.

Ken Lawson's Warlord poster showing a
white man's severed head at his feet also
featured what became the "No justice, no
peace" anthem of the rioters: "Until there
is justice there will be no peace."

CHAPTER 5

SECOND THOUGHTS

The "Law Dog" stood in his corner office on the 15th floor of the tall, square, sugar-box white Kroger Building, overlooking Central Parkway, the dividing line between fragile safety and rock-throwing insanity. It was the morning of the second day, April 10. Ken Lawson, the street-fighter lawyer who had helped provoke the meltdown at City Hall that triggered race riots the day before, was having some second thoughts.

"I could see the rioters coming down Vine Street, just wrecking everything. I was scared," he remembers. "For the next two or three days I just looked out my window. That's when I started to wonder if I'd done something wrong."

Lawson is not a large man, but the former linebacker at Princeton High School plays big. His force of personality fills a room like heavy cologne, made all the more compelling by his deliberately soft-spoken voice that he dials up to a gravelly shout when he gets agitated. His hair is kept short. He sometimes wears an earring to court and once posed for magazine pictures in a baggy, dark-purple zoot-suit, standing alone in a dark street, silhouetted against the city lights like the cover of a pulp-fiction detective novel. His skin is the color of lightly creamed cappuccino, and his office is big enough for half-court hoops. Near the door is his symbol: a life-sized rottweiler statue. A smaller one sits on his desk.

"They represent loyalty and unwillingness to allow anybody to harm those they protect," he explains. "A pit bull or a rottweiler will fight to the death. That's what I'm all about."

He marketed his Law Dog image with an infamous Warlord poster that gave ulcers to the white-shirts-and-wingtips crowd at the courthouse. It showed him on an elaborate African throne, dressed in camouflage

battle fatigues, flanked by music-video models and black-and-brown attack dogs. The severed head of a white man lay at his feet. A similar mural
of Lawson walking rottweilers straining on a leash is painted larger than
life on the front of June Bug's, a barbecue joint in the West End, run by
Lawson's close friend and buddy, George Beatty.

Beatty also runs the Parktown Café nightclub next door to June Bug's,
an address well known to cops in the mid-90s for constant police runs,
gunshots, a police bribery scandal and chronic reports of drug trouble. A
lot of neighbors and cops wanted to shut it down. But instead, with a hard
shove from Beatty's friends on city council, the Parktown was moved and
expanded in 1997 with a generous taxpayer-funded loan of $159,000.

On the streets, Lawson is a genuine folk hero. Among the drug boys,
which is how dealers are proudly known on the streets, he's treated like the
unofficial mayor of the city. The hard cases look up to no one, but even
the baddest bad boys know "what you gonna do when they come for
you"—call Lawson.

Lawson became the best known black lawyer in Cincinnati, the go-to
guy for nearly all media-swarming cases involving black defendants, especially allegations of racial profiling and other civil rights claims—which
often come up sooner or later in a Lawson case.

Before 2001, he was known best for his defense of Cincinnati Reds
superstar Deion Sanders in 1995. Sanders was accused of dragging a cop
with his scooter after the cop tried to stop him as he left the Reds club-
house after a game. Lawson attacked the credibility of the cop's story.
When it was over, the jury found the cop not credible and Sanders not
guilty—and immediately asked Deion for autographs.

Lawson's office walls are decorated with large framed pictures and
news clippings, like the one that shows him with Sanders, arm in arm,
leaving the courtroom victorious. There are framed headlines from his big
cases, and *Cincinnati Magazine* covers featuring flattering profiles. To his
clients, he's the fearless courtroom Rottweiler. To most of the press, he's ad-
mired as a champion of the underdog, a black thorn under the pale, thin
skin of square conservatives. To cops and most of the white community,
he became known as the Johnny Cochran of Cincinnati, always ready to
turn every case into another O.J. trial, never missing a chance to play the
race card from a stacked deck of grievances.

None of those portraits is quite fair. Lawson, like all of us, is more complicated than anything that can be contained behind glass in a picture frame. "I'm a lot more conservative than most people think, especially on social issues," he says. But he also admits, "I have always had a hard time dealing with authority."

Lawson started out as the adopted son of a black couple, and he learned early on that he was not their natural son. "I was lighter color and I was teased a lot," he says. "So I started fighting early."

He had a lot of problems with authority growing up in Cincinnati communities Woodlawn, Avondale and Lincoln Heights. In fourth grade, he hit a teacher. In eighth grade, he was suspended for fighting. At Princeton High School, he was a decent linebacker who liked to hit hard. He still does.

When he graduated from the University of Cincinnati Law School he was already married with kids of his own. He was the first black lawyer hired at the blue-suit, buttoned-down, Queen City Club law firm of Taft-Stettinius, which carries the family name of President Robert Taft and the governor of Ohio during the riots, Bob Taft.

Lawson didn't last long at Taft. But while he was there, he began to track down his biological parents.

He says he found his mother at Tender Mercies, a home for the mentally ill in Over-the Rhine. She was white and Italian. He found out he was born in Longview, a mental hospital that he believes was also used at the time for unwed mothers.

Lawson kept digging. A cousin told him his father was the famous Cincinnati boxer Ezzard Charles. His mother more or less confirmed it by telling him she was close to the boxer known as "The Cincinnati Razor." Charles won the heavyweight title in 1949 by beating Jersey Joe Walcott, and then retained it by beating Joe Louis in 1950. In 1951, Charles lost the title to Walcott. In 1954, he fought Rocky Marciano twice, losing both times in bouts that are now considered boxing classics.

Son of a heavyweight champ.

It fits the Law Dog like one of his tailored courtroom suits. He has the temper and guts to wear it well.

Nearly five years after the riots, he still gets hot when he talks about the way legitimate protests over the shooting of Timothy Thomas were hijacked by young black street thugs, like muggers stealing the champ's silver belt.

"There were people who were truly interested in protesting, demanding no more deaths. And then you had this group that just wanted all hell to break loose."

He first saw them immediately after the eruption of violence and threats at City Hall, when he rode his motorcycle to see the crowd surrounding police headquarters—on Ezzard Charles Drive. "It was a different group. It was the young men from the street corners."

Lawson saw the first broken windows and quickly left. He says he went on the radio each night to urge an end to the violence. "Their criminal actions had nothing to do with police misconduct," he says. "That was just an excuse. For them, it could have been a party out of control, anything. They were just interested in looting and stealing."

He still resents the way the rioters looted his cause, and changed the post-riot focus to "getting in touch with the youth." For days and weeks after the smoke cleared, business, political and media leaders declared that the riots were a "wake-up call" to warn us that Cincinnati had to figure out why the young people were so "troubled."

The problem was not "troubled youth." Even street fighters like Lawson acknowledge that the problem was too many teens and idle 20-something black men who were completely *untroubled* by rioting, beatings, arson and destruction of their own neighborhoods. The problem was an underclass of dropouts and drug boys who grabbed the moment with both hands and ran with it like a pair of looted Air Jordans.

But the "root cause" club was determined to stick to its script, blaming poverty, alienation, lack of jobs and social injustice. "Community dialogue" ensued. A well-intentioned "Common Ground" event arranged by public television and *Enquirer* Managing Editor Rosemary Goudreau was a painfully predictable flop. Various leaders in the black community, whose jobs and agencies subsisted on generosity and kindness from white Cincinnati, remained silent as a few angry militants were handed yet another media bullhorn to broadcast angry accusations of racism and personally attack anyone on their enemies list.

The dialogue became another hostile monologue. As far as reaching youths who rioted, it worked like a radio show for the hearing impaired or Technicolor for the blind. They wanted nothing to do with it.

"The media has a responsibility not to slant things," Lawson said. "We do a good job of keeping our community divided. We do a bad job of constructively criticizing members of our own race—on both sides. It's always, 'Change the city, Mayor Charlie, change the city, City Council.' But just listen to talk radio. We don't want to change ourselves."

Even before the riots, one of Cincinnati's most prominent black leaders, Federal Judge Nathaniel Jones, delivered a speech calling conservative WLW talk radio "trash, profanity and filth."

But muzzled by political correctness, no leaders, black or white, did the same to put "Da Buzz" on front street, or call out its hosts for encouraging and spreading ignorance, lies, rumors and paranoia. No accusation was too far-fetched or absurd for hosts such as Jonathan Love, whose father owned the station. No racially divisive rant accusing cops of hunting down black men or abusing suspects was too inflammatory for the Al Jazeera of Cincinnati.

Cops, council members and the mayor all blamed WDBZ as one of the leading instigators of violence during the riots.

Jones may have had a point about WLW, where hosts such as Bill Cunningham have sometimes been over-the-top provocative, mocking boycotters and black homicide victims. "Where is the black leadership when there is racial violence against white America?" Cunningham asked on the radio on April 11. "If there was a white mob beating up on black people because of the color of their skin, I'd be just as tough on them."

But compared to the urban legends spread on WDBZ, where "racist cop" was often used as one word, even Cunningham was as mild as vanilla pudding.

Lawson is almost alone among leaders in the black community when he criticizes WDBZ. He's still a pit bull. But his bark has changed pitch slightly. He now realizes that he started a protest—and a riot broke out. And his city will never be quite the same.

Like nearly everything else, Cincinnati should have seen it coming.

Five years before the riots, in 1996, Lawson took the case of Darryll Price, who died after a struggle with officers. Lawson went on the radio and said the cops "beat him to death with their billy clubs." Two autopsies from separate coroners showed Price died from "agitated delirium with restraint," not from a beating by the cops.

Critics warned then that Lawson was trying to incite a riot.

Lawson fired back: "My comments could not have started a riot. Period. I find it hard to believe that (police) kill people in custody, but it's my comments that could cause a riot."

A 1998 *Enquirer* profile of Lawson, headlined "Junkyard Dog of Justice," included another prophetic quote, this time from Hamilton County Prosecutor Joe Deters.

"On a personal level, I like Ken," Deters said. "I think he is a good attorney."

But then Deters expressed what many suspect is the worst side of Lawson: "He has a unique opportunity because he reaches a segment of the black community that even many black leaders don't reach," Deters said. "The only thing in my mind that keeps Ken from being a great lawyer and a great citizen is his reluctance to relate to his constituency the realities of the court system. And in many respects I think that is divisive, and he knows better."

So on April 9, as Lawson sat at City Hall while the mob screamed hysterically all around him, city officials thought he knew better then, too—that he was deliberately aggravating the volatile hostility and frustration by asking for details that could not be made public without compromising the investigation of the shooting.

Lawson's most violent outburst came when Assistant Chief Ron Twitty said as much: "I know Mr. Lawson knows this."

"Don't tell me what I know," Lawson yelled back. "You run that on someone else. Don't you ever tell me what I know."

Lawson said later, "All we wanted to know was what Roach's first statement was," he says. "What did he say? There was no way that could interfere with any investigation. The statement was already made. Prosecutors do that all the time. Someone confesses in the back of a cruiser and they come right out and say 'The suspect confessed, here's what he said.' In this case, the answer was 'It just went off.' That's what Roach said. That's all we wanted to hear, and when Tarbell finally told us and answered that question at the meeting, that's when everyone left."

That sounds reasonable. But lawyers who have handled cases against cops say Lawson was wrong. Police officers are protected by the Garrity Rule established by the U.S. Supreme Court. If they are ordered by commanding officers to make a statement, that statement cannot be used against them in court.

So what Roach told Captain Paul Humphries—the acting chief that night who was first on the scene—was probably covered by the Garrity Rule. Roach and his FOP lawyers could argue in court that any statement to Humphries was not admissible. And by the time Chief Streicher and other city officials attended the April 9 meeting, Roach was saying he thought Thomas was reaching for a weapon.

If the Police Chief repeated Roach's first statement in that meeting, there was a good chance it would lose its value in court and the case against Roach would indeed be jeopardized. Twitty was right. And from the rearview mirror five years later, it looks like Lawson's violent denial may have been a chemical reaction to contact with the truth.

Asked later if he regrets what he did at City Hall that day, his answer was a surprise. Things could have been different, he said. But it was Mayor Charlie Luken who fumbled and lost the keys to peace.

"The mayor's staff called Angela Leisure that day, asking to come to her home and answer questions. The press was there waiting. He didn't show up. Then we find out he was at the council meeting and that's when we went down there.

"Angela and I would have never showed up there if the mayor had made his appointment. You might have had a more heated council meeting than usual. But that's it."

Luken said there is no truth to Lawson's story. "I met with her and (NAACP leader) Kweise Mfume later. There was never a request to meet with her. I tried to call her several times, but I was rebuffed. She was very abrupt. I would have gladly gone to her home, but there was never any request for that."

Lawson still thinks about his own role in ramping up the anger. "Lynch came and whispered in my ear and asked, 'Should we lock the doors and make sure nobody leaves until we get an answer?' I told him I can't say that because I'm an attorney."

So Lynch went ahead and did it, and the mob hysteria crossed a line from screaming tantrum to genuine menace. In that moment, the riots were born. In that moment, a pastor incited violence. In that moment, the thugs who were already in the room hijacked the protests and turned the justified crusade for an explanation into lawless mayhem.

Whatever second thoughts Lawson had on that second day, they are mostly gone now.

"Sometimes you don't fear any man or woman because you know, even if you are wrong, that in your heart what you're doing is right and God is with you. So the answer is no. I don't think it was wrong."

Councilman Cecil Thomas headed up the
Law and Public Safety Committee in 2006.
Thomas, who waded into the riots to urge
peace as director of the Cincinnati Human
Relations Commission, was elected to
Council in 2005.

CHAPTER 6

BROKEN SIDEWALKS

Cincinnati's most famous landmark, the Roebling Suspension Bridge, looks like a copy of the Brooklyn Bridge—but it's the other way around. John Roebling overcame critics and an interruption by the Civil War to stretch his wire rope cables over soaring towers and lift his first "impossible" suspension bridge over the Ohio River, connecting Cincinnati and Covington, Kentucky in 1866— 27 years before the his Brooklyn Bridge was opened to traffic. His engineering marvel bridged two cities, two states and two worlds, as it crossed the immeasurable gap that separated slave-state Kentucky from Ohio, which became a free state when the Northwest Ordinance prohibited slavery in 1787, seventy-six years before President Abraham Lincoln's Emancipation Proclamation.

> **Article 6 of the Northwest Ordinance**: "There shall be neither slavery nor involuntary servitude in the said territory, otherwise than in the punishment of crimes whereof the party shall have been duly convicted: Provided, always, That any person escaping into the same, from whom labor or service is lawfully claimed in any one of the original States, such fugitive may be lawfully reclaimed and conveyed to the person claiming his or her labor or service as aforesaid."

It was that second half, "Provided, always . . . such fugitive may be lawfully reclaimed," that caused Cincinnati's first major riot. The pro-slavery riot began on April 11, 1836—165 years to the day before the race riots of 2001. According to "The History of Hamilton County and Cincinnati, Ohio" published in 1894, black families' houses were burned and they were "shot down like dogs." It went on for days until martial law was declared. Three months later, a rioting mob tried to burn the press of a local abolitionist publisher.

As slave-hunters crossed the Ohio to chase down runaways, Cincinnati became a human-rights hotbed for radicals in the Abolitionist movement. Records show claims for 300 fugitive slaves per year who had fled to Cincinnati—not including the ones that escaped. The north shore of the river was soon honeycombed with tunnels, hidden rooms, secret basements and hidden attics—portals for the Underground Railroad.

For slaves gazing north across the Ohio River from Kentucky, or south from Ohio toward the families and friends they had left behind, the river was as wide as an ocean—as wide as the infinite distance between heaven and hell.

÷÷÷

Sometimes the Ohio River is a froggy green, the color of a lazy, drifting Huck Finn summer. Sometimes it's steely blue, corrugated by the winter wind into miniature whitecaps. Most of the time it's the color of creamed coffee or a chocolate-milkshake, sliding by like a placid, gentle giant that moves slowly on the surface but contains the hidden, effortless strength to carry entire houses on its shoulders in a swirling flood.

And always, it's a boundary that measures difference, a barrier that separates North and South. The river gave Ohio its name—"beautiful River"—from the Shawnee Indians who crossed it to their sacred hunting grounds in Kentucky. It's a superhighway of water for antique wedding-cake paddle-wheelers and modern river freight trains of coal-heaped barges. The river is so big it influences the weather and the human climate on both sides.

It takes a great bridge to cross a great river—and the Roebling Bridge has no equal on the Ohio River. It's a spider web of blue-painted cables, stretched like elegant schooner rigging between arched stone piers capped by gold ornaments that look from a distance like crosses. The towers that make "saddles" for the sequoia-girthed cables look like triumphal gateways. Or from another perspective, they can look like the draw-bridged entrance over the moat of a castle.

It's a marvel of architectural beauty. Skeptical crowds expected it to collapse and splash into the river when it opened, but 140 years later it still hums under the tires of Hondas, Cadillacs, Chryslers and

Toyota pickups that were not even dreamed of when it was built. Illuminated at night, it's a fairytale bridge that joins the Emerald City skyline of Cincinnati to a blanket of jeweled lights in Kentucky, arching over a black mirror of water that reflects both sides in shimmering colors from a treasure chest.

Everywhere in Cincinnati, the suspension bridge shows up in paintings, on key chains, brochures, posters and postcards. It's a landmark—but also a fitting symbol of the past and present. It reminds us that Cincinnati is always working on a bridge to span the gap between black and white, north and south, future and past. That, too, is a work of beauty, representing all the best intentions of a city's most noble nature. But like the Roebling, our carefully engineered bridge of commissions, social services and programs is designed to arch above the muddy waters of everyday life, so we can cross over and back without getting our feet wet in the turbulent emotions of race conflict.

Race issues have spawned an elaborate choreography of communication. Place one foot wrong, and careers, even corporations, can be blown up by land mines of alleged "racism" or "insensitivity." Step out of line in the wrong neighborhood, and the cops are waiting with steel bracelets and an all-expenses-paid vacation in the Justice Center.

It's no wonder so many have learned to loathe the enforced "diversity training" and politically correct "dialogue."

But here's a surprise: if we get away from the tangle of crossed cables and stone walls of race anger, and simply wade into the muddy riverbanks and meet each other as individuals, not groups, we can discover that the gap that looks as wide as the Ohio River is really as narrow as a bump in an uneven, cracked sidewalk.

÷ ÷ ÷

"When you walk around Music Hall, the sidewalks are smooth and new," says Cecil Thomas, a former Cincinnati Police officer who was director of the Cincinnati Human Relations Commission during the riots. "As soon as you get into Over-the-Rhine, now you've got big chunks of cement missing, or big cracks where one side sticks up higher. Kids can't roller skate on that. It's a 'who cares?' attitude. That's why people get frustrated."

Talk-show host Lincoln Ware, the voice of black radio on WDBZ, brought up the same grievance. "If you can use our tax money to fix up your areas, why can't we get ours fixed?

"You can tell the difference when you cross that line. On Opening Day, it was funny. I'm watching the Reds Parade, and all the black folks are out on the sidewalks in Over-the-Rhine. Then as you go south, it starts getting lighter, and when you cross Central Avenue, suddenly it's all white."

Thomas and Ware are old enough to have seen the Cincinnati riots in the late 60s, then again in 2001. In 1968, riots broke out in Avondale on April 8, four days after the assassination of Dr. Martin Luther King. Two were killed, 220 were arrested and $3 million in property damage was reported.

"Over the years, blacks felt like they were getting a raw deal," Ware said, sitting in his office at WDBZ across from City Hall. "We couldn't get in on the contracts or the jobs. The whites had control and we couldn't break that barrier, all the way back to the 60s and 70s. Look at Burnett Avenue in Avondale. It still looks the same way, like downtown Beirut. It hasn't changed since the riots in 1968."

Thomas sees Cincinnati as a moated castle, not a welcoming gateway. "When you look at what really was the cause of the unrest, it goes way back to problems that never really were addressed, they were just painted over. It's like a cancer that's in remission, but never gets cured. It goes back to the 60s."

He blames the construction of I-75 that split up healthy neighborhoods in Over-the-Rhine and the West End like a wide river of concrete. It walled off and divided both neighborhoods, turning them into isolated pools of poverty, despair and crime. And the city soon turned its back on both, he said.

"When you ignore the quality of life, you create an illness that only gets worse. There were warning signs. A strained relationship between black citizens and the police. A high school dropout rate among African-American males at over 50 percent. Large concentrations of poverty in a small geographical area. Poor housing. Poverty."

"When you go through those streets, you roll up your windows and hit the lock button," Thomas says. "We ignore it and say, 'Oh, God, I'm so glad I don't live down here.'"

Both Ware and Thomas describe the poverty pockets of Cincinnati like neighborhoods that time forgot. Neglected and ignored, hidden by highways, places where government gave up.

Looking back on the riots, both men admit that many in the black community never spoke up because they secretly supported the rioters and the boycott that followed. Go deeper, and both will almost admit to being there themselves.

"There's a feeling," Ware said, "that a lot of things never would have happened without the riots. People say 'Look what we gotta do to get something done.' "

Yet both also admit they were shocked and scared by what they saw in 2001.

"The people who are gonna sell drugs, commit violence, kill each other in turf wars, I don't know what you're gonna do about that," says Ware, a former Marine, shaking his head.

"I saw people driving down the street shooting big guns, we're talking 9 mm, long-barrel pistols. The lawlessness of people was what scared me most. I wondered how long before they start shooting at me? They didn't look like people from the neighborhood. That was what scared me most. It was frightening."

Thomas said, "You had those who seized the moment to do things that would be unacceptable in any expression of anger or frustration. Rev. Lynch—he sure enough lost control of the people who surrounded him, and that opened the door."

Nobody has been a tougher critic of the Cincinnati Police than Thomas, who was one of the first cops to file a complaint about discrimination against black officers. But he also blames black leaders and the black community.

A few months after the riots, police chased a suspect into the parking lot of the church where boycott leader the Rev. Damon Lynch III was pastor. As they were putting cuffs on the suspect, an angry crowd gathered and the cops asked Lynch to help settle people down. Lynch answered, "That's not my job."

Thomas says it *is* Lynch's job, and the job of everyone to support the police when they clean up crime that infests black neighborhoods. "I told the Reverend Lynch, 'Look, folks, you can't have it both ways. We've got drugs out here, people killing each other. You have to support the police even if they make minor mistakes. We've got to realize they are not perfect. We've got to get back to a time when lawlessness will not be tolerated. Everybody in the city has one common agenda: we don't want crime."

"I refuse to accept that Cincinnati is racist," says Thomas, who has known racism the way a cancer patient knows pain. "I just don't buy into it, because of the goodwill in the hearts of the majority of this community."

Michael Howard is about the same age as Ware and Thomas. He grew up on the streets of Cincinnati's poorest black neighborhoods, the West End and Over-the-Rhine, and he regularly walks those streets today.

Everyone knows him as "Nitti," his street name borrowed from Al Capone's hit man, Frank Nitti. Howard wore it like a badge of honor during the 60s and 70s, when he was a feared drug gang enforcer and Golden Gloves boxer in the West End. But today, they call him Nitti with a hug and a smile—and Michael always stops to return a smile and bear-hug embrace to his friends, or offer help to his street family of ex-cons, single-moms, crack addicted prostitutes, homeless winos and the empty husks of men sucked dry by heroin. Now they know Howard as a new man who follows Christ and walks with Jesus while too many others—even church leaders—only talk the talk.

"People in these neighborhoods have no respect for Lynch," he says, walking the West End where he grew up. "They know he's never around when you need help. He just shows up for the photo ops."

Howard is director of Justice Watch, a halfway house for paroled convicts who are struggling like he once did before God turned his life around and he became one of the first ex-cons to graduate from the University of Cincinnati.

Howard is different. And not just in the way Christians are different. He's different because he is not afraid to demonstrate and demand personal accountability in a culture that would rather hide behind victimhood and blame someone else.

While others talk about how things haven't changed, he works to change them. While others talk about how things used to be, Howard says, "Get over it. Ain't nobody holding the black man down but himself. Look in the mirror."

While others pick up and carry the burden of poverty and historic racism like a badge, Howard says black families need to drop it and stop blaming whites and the police so they can start fixing their own problems—starting with families where children have only one parent if they have any around at all.

Along the broken sidewalks of Over-the-Rhine and the West End, past the liquor stores, drug dealers, prostitutes, crackheads, pimps and thugs, "Hell Town" has been painted in a red-sprayed scrawl like splattered blood on the weathered boards covering empty windows on abandoned buildings.

"Urban Taliban," Howard says, pointing to a street-corner group of drug boys in saggy cellblock jeans and red do-rag bandanas, clustered like grapes on the crime vine. "Look at that," he says in disgusted disbelief as they trade baggies of "rock" for wads of cash. "We are poisoning ourselves."

Howard walks through Cincinnati's heart of darkness. But he also walks on the white side of the street at churches, social events, public meetings, in downtown offices and restaurants.

And occasionally, like something out of the corner of an eye, the ghost of racism can be glimpsed. It's a stare that lasts a split-second too long, a look of surprise, eyes with questions the lips won't speak. To whites, it's nearly always hidden and invisible. They don't believe in ghosts. For blacks, it has jumped out of the closet in all its ugliness too many times. They know it's there and they think white people must be naive, lying or blind.

Men like Thomas and Ware are right about the past—but it's so easy to forget and ignore. Too many consciences have become scarred and calloused by the feel-gooders and race hustlers who have bled white guilt as dry as stale crackers, who cry "racist" wolf because it's easier than defending the extreme crime rate among young black men or just admitting "I disagree."

But still . . . anyone brave enough to get their feet wet in that muddy river can see the other side a lot clearer. From there, it's possible to envision a future in which men like Michael Howard lead the way across the bridge to freedom and leave behind the shackles of bigotry and bitterness.

History is as solid as the stone piers of the Roebling Bridge, sunk deep into the bedrock of Cincinnati. It's part of the landscape.

But the future can still be changed.

÷ ÷ ÷

A museum sits at the foot of the Roebling Bridge on the Ohio riverbank today. The National Underground Railroad Freedom Center is a $110 million symbol of racial reconciliation, funded by taxpayers, local corporations and private donations to honor Cincinnati's role in freedom from slavery. Many hoped it would counter the city's national negative reputation from the riots as the "racist" capital of America. But that's asking too much—like pinning hopes on the Roebling Bridge to reunite North and South.

On the other hand, it's about time we recognized that those chapters in our history belong in a museum—not as baggage we carry into the future.

It's time to cross that river together.

A gang of rioters climbed on top of
stopped cars in a blocked intersection on
April 10, the first full day of violence, as
white motorists were dragged from their
cars and beaten.

CHAPTER 7

GREAT RIOT WEATHER

The third full day of the riots, April 12, dawned like a fresh June bride. Perfect. Beautiful. By 8 a.m. the spring sunshine sparkled on broken glass in the streets of Over-the-Rhine and warmed gentle southerly breezes to a T-shirt-comfortable 67 degrees. The forecast was clear, sunny and unseasonably hot. By 10 a.m. it was 71 and the mercury was still climbing like the lazy plumes of smoke from burned-out shops in the war zone. As the afternoon began, clouds slowly assembled to crowd the sky and pull a modest shade over the sun. At 3 p.m. the heat peaked at a sticky 84, and April 12 felt like something misplaced on the calendar, a day meant for July that was dropped in the wrong file. Rumors of possible thunderstorms gave the city fleeting hope that God might do what all the prayers, preachers and police could not, and finally douse the fires of hate that were gnawing at the heart of the city.

"It was such a beautiful day. Great riot weather. We couldn't get a drop of rain. I was praying for rain," said Mayor Charlie Luken, looking out a tall window in his first-floor office in the southeast corner of City Hall. "I wanted to go out in the street and do a rain dance for rain."

The mercy rains never came. Instead, Cincinnati got another perfect day for riots.

Luken remembers how he sat in his office under the tall ceiling, alone behind his large oak desk with a portable radio playing nearby as he tried to work. "I was listening to the crap on the Buzz. It came very close to inciting."

On the black radio station WDBZ, Ken Lawson was stirring up trouble, Luken said.

"I thought his behavior was reprehensible. He was on the radio, calling people who were rioting 'soljahs.' It was just awful. They were talking as if the rioters were doing God's work."

On "Da Buzz," the voices were calling for Luken to resign. And when he switched to the conservative white side of local talk radio down the dial on WLW, there was Fraternal Order of Police President Keith Fangman—also telling Luken to resign.

Luken ignored both extremes. He had other problems.

"I call it the day the music died. It was the day that the city manager form of government was proven for all time to be ineffective," Luken said.

Luken had been watching in frustration as City Manager John Shirey turned off the lights, closed his office next door and went home by 5:30 each night, just as the city was having another convulsion. "I would call him and tell him to 'Get your ass back here.' Sometimes he would. I think he didn't understand the gravity of it."

Shirey was good at fixing the plumbing of city government, but he was helpless in a flood of violence, Luken said. Shirey's toolbox contained nothing for a riot.

"Finally, when an officer got shot I said, 'I'm going to have a press conference and declare a curfew. You can show up and support me or not.' The authority ran to the city manager. But I just said, 'If you don't like it, get out of the way.'"

That day was a turning point. It was the day Luken made his boldest move for control, and his biggest mistake.

Most people who don't like Charlie Luken have probably never met him. He is Cincinnati's version of the "fortunate one" in the old Creedence Clearwater song—a Congressman's son. His father, Democrat Tom Luken, was known from Capitol Hill to City Hall for seismic eruptions of his volcanic temper. Charlie came from a long line of Lukens who were lucky in politics. The son who followed his father into the family business was born in 1951 and attended Purcell, a Catholic high school, then Notre Dame University and University of Cincinnati Law School. He became a city councilman in 1981, and then over the next two decades he rose to mayor, congressman, local TV news anchorman and mayor again in 1999. In April 2001, his grip on the levers of the city seemed so solid the Republican Party could not find a candidate to run against him—a mistake they regretted bitterly when the next election rolled around and Luken came in second in the post-riot primary to an independent TV reporter. But Luken had never lost an election, and it seemed like he had never even lost his cool.

Charlie Luken is affable and can be disarmingly matter-of-fact candid. It's a style that makes it easy to forget his skill as a calculating political artist. Even Republican Party leaders honor him with the label, "One of the most gifted politicians Cincinnati has ever seen."

He has a dry, sarcastic sense of humor, and he's not afraid to turn it on himself and other council members. He's slim, of medium height, with all-American clean-cut good looks. His round, wire-frame glasses and medium-length, neatly styled hair make him look like a trustworthy TV doctor or a popular high school English teacher. He dresses sharp, runs meetings efficiently in his bright Brooks Brothers ties and white shirt-sleeves, plays low-handicap golf and commands attention with the steady and unflappable I'm-in-control voice of an airline pilot, confidently flipping switches and checking the dials of city government.

Luken's way of speaking bluntly would get a less likeable, less skilled politician in deep trouble. But Luken was never in trouble. He was blessed.

"I kinda glided through life. People always said I had a star because I was so lucky."

But by Thursday, April 12, 2001, all that had changed. The famous four-leaf-clover Luken luck had locked its office door and gone home.

The day before, Luken had gone on CNN. In response to a question, he replied in words that soon became national news and locally infamous: "There's a great deal of frustration within the community, which is understandable. We've had way too many deaths in our community at the hands of Cincinnati police."

÷ ÷ ÷

To the cops in the street, that statement was more painful than the rain of rocks and bottles they waded into in Over-the-Rhine while working 16-hour shifts in the riot zone.

FOP President Fangman vividly remembers jumping into a windowless van on the first big night of violence. "We didn't even know where we were going."

It turned out to be Findlay Market, where the small group of rattled cops was dumped out and just stood there, frozen in disbelief by the scene in front of them. "Three businesses were engulfed in flames. Three cars were on fire. All the dumpsters were just engulfed in flames. There were gunshots everywhere—these thugs were celebrating the riots by shooting into the air. We were not prepared for this."

Devereoes, a store specializing in hip-hop fashions and the latest hoops sneakers endorsed by NBA superstars, "was filled with looters like ants," Fangman recalls. "There were so many it looked like an anthill. All of us were stunned. We couldn't believe what we were seeing."

"I immediately thought of the 1992 Rodney King riots in L.A. Before I was a police officer, I saw this video on CNN, and there were these cops just standing there while looters were carrying TVs and stereos out of a Sears store, and I was outraged. The cops said, 'There are just two of us and 500 of them. What do you expect us to do? We would get ripped to shreds.' And then, when I saw it myself, I understood what they meant. All we could do was shoot beanbag shotguns and try to disperse the looters, but they would just move to the other end of the block and keep on looting. It was a nightmare. I saw this guy running out of one of the shops carrying a giant ham. Findlay Market was destroyed. An ATM machine was cracked open like an egg. It was a nightmare."

After a night like that, Fangman and the other cops working 16-hour shifts headed for their stations to go home to snatch a few hours of sleep—and heard the news that the mayor was on national TV, blaming them.

"Here was Luken on CNN, essentially apologizing for the rioters," said Fangman. "Our officers were just outraged. He could have nipped that in the bud and supported our police. He could have said our police were doing a fantastic job. Instead, he says this and the national media just ran out there with it, like 'Here's proof, the mayor admits the police are responsible for the deaths of 15 black men.' Why didn't he go over the 15 deaths and tell them what really happened? Why didn't he say the 15 black men who were killed were trying to kill our officers with guns, knives, a brick and a board with nails in it?"

Asked about it later, Luken ruefully admitted, "I wish to hell I had never said that. Part of it was taken out of context. I actually also said I was not blaming anyone, I was not saying whose fault it was. But that one stands out as one I would love to take back."

He knew better, Luken admits. "I was aware of the numbers. I had been on WDBZ with Damon Lynch on Sunday, and I remember him talking about these 15 black men murdered by police, and I wondered at the time, 'What the hell is that, where did it come from?' I'd never heard about it."

So on Monday, Luken asked for research on the number of deaths by police. And what he found was that Fangman was right. "Twelve of the fifteen had weapons. All but two or three were clearly justified."

But it was too late for corrections or clarifications. Fangman, flanked by 50 red-eyed, battle-fatigued cops who had worked all night, held a press conference to demand a curfew and set the record straight.

Like salt in the wounds of Luken's statement, there was more bad news: A cop had been shot at 11 p.m. the night before, while pushing back rock-throwing rioters near Green and Vine streets. Officer Andrew Nogueira was miraculously saved when the bullet bounced off his belt buckle. The shooter, identified only as a 50-something black man, was never found.

Today, Nogueira just smiles and shrugs it off like it was no big deal. He still gets ribbed by other SWAT cops about it. He sums it all up in a single sentence: "There were no rules for them."

Cops have to joke about things like that or they'd get the shakes every time they strap on a bullet-proof vest. But it was a very big deal. Immediately after the shooting of Nogueira, M-16s were issued. But because one side did have rules, none was ever fired during the riots.

"I remember responding to Lynn Street the day Andy was shot," said Lieutenant Doug Ventre, commander of the CPD SWAT Team. "There was a guy breaking into a pony keg. He had blood all over his hands, they were all cut up, but we grabbed him. And then down on Findlay a group of people standing in the shadows started shooting at us. Bullets were hitting the wall right over our heads," he said, slowly shaking his head, like a man who has seen something he still can't believe.

Ventre and his rapid-response teams spent their days hitting hot-spots. They would pile into cruisers in riot gear and rush to a burning store or some trapped motorist who had been pulled from his car and was being beaten in the street. They would disperse the rioters with beanbag shotguns, then get back in the cars and get out fast, before the crowd had a chance to swell and swallow them up.

"We came across people who had been pulled from their cars and beaten, and we'd ask, 'What the hell are you doing down here?' And these young kids would say, 'I just wanted to see what was going on.' We had a bunch of people who got the hell kicked out of them just because they wanted to see what a riot looked like."

Ventre and other police officials say more than 30 white people were beaten by blacks. In one case, *The Cincinnati Enquirer* reported, a light-skinned black woman was being dragged from her car and beaten until someone recognized her and stopped the rioters by yelling "She's black."

"It hurts," said the woman, Roslyn Jones, a 28-year-old mom on her way home from an evening class. "My own people couldn't even recognize me. They didn't even look long enough to see. The first piece of white skin they saw, they hit it."

The white victims were not so lucky. Most were rescued by cops and paramedics and taken to emergency rooms for stitches and treatment of lacerations and contusions.

÷÷÷

But through it all, while many news stories used Luken's remarks to confirm and spread the rioters' stories that the Cincinnati Police were running amok and killing young black men, the cops did not shoot back once, even as bullets flew at them and around them.

"The thing that saved this city is the beanbag shotgun," Ventre said. "There would have been a lot more injuries if we had to go toe-to-toe with rioters and couldn't stand back 60 or 70 feet away and shoot beanbags."

Ventre compares the small, square beanbag projectile to a pitched fast-ball. But because beanbags have the aerodynamics of a throw-pillow, they can be unpredictable and inaccurate. "But if you had a baseball glove you could catch it, or you could step out of the way," he said.

Late in the afternoon of April 12, a mob of rioters massed at 12th and Vine, heading for the downtown business district, Ventre said. "They actually charged our police line. A big whoop went up and here they came. Our guys stood our ground and engaged with beanbag shotguns. The assault was pushed back by cops with beanbags."

Pictures in the newspaper showed young rioters pulling up shirt sleeves to display bruises from beanbags or non-lethal rubber bullets. They showed shirtless youths in do-rags and bandana outlaw masks, climbing right out of their loose hip-hop jeans as they vaulted a fence to escape. Reports made it sound like the cops just randomly opened fire with beanbags. No mention was made that they were laying their lives on the line to protect the downtown business district—including the TV stations and newspapers.

"The fact that people were being savagely beaten because they were white never got any media play," Fangman said. "There is definitely a significant majority in the media, local and national, who love to bash the police and characterize us as racist racial profilers."

Ventre seems likewise mystified. Noguiera could have picked out any knucklehead in the crowd of rioters to blame for the shooting. But he didn't. "Because of Andy's integrity, we made no arrest," Ventre said.

"We never fired a lethal round during the whole thing," Ventre said. "Andy was back at work the next day. He could have taken a long vacation on the city for that. But he went right back to work."

So did Fangman. He used his press conference the next day to point to pictures on the wall behind him at the FOP hall—stark, black-and-white photos that showed most of more than 100 Cincinnati cops killed in the line of duty since 1846. Nearly all of the recent police fatalities were killed by black men, he said to the gathered press. "I told them 90 percent of the violent crime, 95 percent of the assaults on cops, 93 percent of the murders and 90 percent of the rapes in the city are done by black men, who account for 40 percent of the population.

"But I asked, would it be fair to say all black males are predisposed to kill cops? No, that would be racist and unfair. It would be an inflammatory statement—just as unfair as saying fifteen black men were murdered by police, which was all over the national and local media."

Fangman says demands by the FOP for a curfew worked. On April 12, Luken announced that anyone found on the streets between 8 p.m. and 6 a.m. would be arrested.

But Luken said his mind was already made up on the curfew after hearing the chilling police radio call late the night before: "Shots fired. Officer down."

At his own press conferences, Luken compared the gunshots in the street to "something you would expect to hear in Beirut."

"I'd been arguing for a curfew for 36 hours, but the city manager and police chief thought it was a situation that would resolve itself. I'm not sure an earlier curfew would have brought about a different result—like, 'It's 8 p.m., time to stop looting and pillaging.'"

Fangman says the city dragged its feet too long trying to be politically correct and "sensitive" to the rioters. "They were walking on eggshells, trying not to offend Damon Lynch. They hoped if they played nice, it would stop. But the more they played nice, the worse it got. If they had called a curfew that first night, the rioting would have stopped right there."

Luken disagrees. He believes the rioters just got fatigued. "They ran out of steam."

Lynch and others accused the city of targeting black neighborhoods with the curfew, while failing to enforce it in white neighborhoods outside the riot zones. Police said that was nonsense. The curfew worked. After 8 p.m., police picked up anyone who even looked like a rioter. "But there was a hell of a lot of restraint on the curfew," Ventre said. "With a lot of people, we just took them home. That was never reported, either."

÷÷÷

Luken sat in his office where he had listened to talk-shows demanding his resignation during the riots, and looked inward and back, like someone who has made an uneasy peace with the past. "It was unfair," he said. "But it was all unfair."

Everything was changed that week in April. "More than anything, it taught me about myself," he said.

"If you want to blame me for something, that's fine, but at least give me the authority. They go back and say I should have stayed at the (Law and Public Safety) meeting or I should have called the curfew earlier. But I think I handled it as adroitly as anyone could have."

He paused, and added, "Everybody wants someone to blame. How about if we start by blaming the rioters?"

Luken says he nearly walked away from the mayor's office that year, but he couldn't abide the image in his mind of a "Luken Quits" headline. So he ran again, survived a primary defeat to an opponent who had never held public office, and won re-election the following November.

He also got the authority he wanted as Cincinnati's first "strong mayor" since the 1920s. With a charter change approved by voters, the city manager's tangled lines of authority that led nowhere, like cut wires, were yanked out. Three years into his second term, Luken finally decided that he would not run for mayor again. He'd had enough.

"I'm a better public servant than I was. I always heard it, but never really understood what it meant before. But it's true. At the end of the day, there is nobody in the mirror but yourself."

At the end of the third full day of riots, Luken was listening to a police radio. Every afternoon, the evil would come creeping back, poking its ugly head around the corners in static-crackling reports on police scanners, as the rioters began to gather like rain clouds. "At 4 o'clock every day, I'd hear those cops come on their radios and say there are 30 here at such and such corner, 40 over there . . . It was just horrible. Awful."

Then on that night of April 12, something amazing happened. The curfew somehow worked. The next morning dawned like the days before, beautiful. Perfect. Hot. But Friday the 13th turned out to be Cincinnati's lucky day.

The riots were over at last. Cincinnati began sweeping up the broken glass. The city's slow, painful resurrection began. It was Good Friday.

A rioter wearing a bandana walked past a burning store on Elder Street in Findlay Market on April 10. One cop said the Market looked like an anthill of looters.

CHAPTER 8

"15 BLACK MEN"

O n a cloudy morning in June under an overcast sky the color of dirty sheets, four men in Dockers shorts and open-necked, pastel knit shirts embroidered with polo players and alligators stood on the tee-box overlooking a Par 3 at Legendary Run golf course in southern Clermont County, several miles east of downtown Cincinnati in the rolling hills and horse pastures that once belonged to convicted S&L tycoon Marvin Warner. They could have been almost any Saturday morning foursome on any golf course in Cincinnati—a G.E. guy, a newsman, a lawyer and a manager at Procter & Gamble. Who they were is not as important as how they reacted as they watched their safe, boring, Midwestern streets of Cincinnati—their downtown "office"—turn into a war zone.

As they stood on a hilltop overlooking the fairway, the land gently rippled and folded like an unmade bed. Just beyond the southern horizon lay the banks of the Ohio River, where paddle-wheelers used to blow their falsetto whistles and play circus-parade calliopes, and farmers would stop and lift their heads from the plow or the disc and dream of distances that only a big river knows.

The emerald fairways and lighter mint-pastel greens were still sugarglazed with dew, leaving darker outlines of spidery ball tracks and footprints as clear as black cutout dance steps at an Arthur Murray Studio. As the men waited for the group ahead to putt out and move on to the next tee, conversation turned from political rumors and stale lawyer jokes to the recent riots.

"What the hell is going on?" Ed, the Procter & Gamble guy asked. The rest of the group knew what he meant. It was a rhetorical question. He worked downtown. He knew very well what the hell was going on. He was just giving voice to the confusion and worry they all felt about the future of the city and the unspoken fear that polluted the city like a toxic spill.

"Shoot 'em all and let God sort 'em out," joked Greg the lawyer with a tee in the corner of his mouth.

"Hell, I don't blame them for burning up the city if the cops killed fifteen black kids," said Ray the G.E. guy.

At that, the conversation pancaked flat, like a Titlest cratered in a bunker. After a long pause to stare silently at their shoes and the foursome ahead doing its slow plumb-bob Master's Tournament waltz on the green, a couple of guys grudgingly nodded and the lawyer wondered, "What the hell?"

"That's a load of crap," Greg finally said. "All but a couple of those so-called 'victims' were shooting at cops or trying to kill someone. Only a couple of the shootings were even questionable, and even those guys violently resisted arrest."

But the story was too complicated to explain in the time it takes to three-putt. After all, they'd seen it repeatedly over and over in the local papers and ratified in the national media: 15 black men killed by the Cincinnati Police.

A lie can play 18 holes before the truth gets its clubs out of the trunk. And this lie was the Tiger Woods of media mythology. How could the ordinary truth hope to compete if even these 40-something, successful, well-informed professionals—guys with SUVs parked in suburban driveways, kids in private schools and half-acre lawns to mow on Saturday mornings—had already made up their minds?

Time Magazine called Cincinnati "a model of racial unfairness."

NAACP leader Kweise Mfume said Cincinnati was "the belly of the beast" of police violence against black men.

Boycotters, protesters, editorial writers, social workers, local politicians, college professors, civil rights activists and all the other charter members of the Root Cause Club had already made up their minds. The "unrest," as they liked to call it, was a justified and overdue reaction to years of racial injustice, poverty and police brutality.

Even the mayor had announced to CNN during the riots that, "We've had way too many deaths in our community at the hands of Cincinnati police."

An editor at *The Cincinnati Enquirer* boasted in a corporate memo about the paper's riot coverage, saying Cincinnati Police "had 15 African-American men die in its custody since 1996."

How's a busy guy in Suburba-topia, with a mortgage and two car payments, supposed to argue with all of that while his friends are waiting for him to tee up and shank one into the weeds?

Like most junk-food stories, the "15 Black Men" headline contained a jelly filling of truth. But the rest of it was nutritionally empty sponge cake and shiny cellophane wrappers.

The myth was probably born on a Sunday morning on June 27, 1997, with a splashy big series in the *Enquirer*. "Misuse of Force" the headline shouted, right next to a shocking, gut-wrenching photo of a black man dripping streams of blood over his face from a head wound.

"Almost always, police perform admirably—even heroically—under difficult and sometimes life-threatening conditions," it began in a note from Editor Lawrence Beaupre. "However . . . "

A lot of cops thought it looked like classic contest journalism—like the sensational Chiquita stories that later wrecked Beaupre's career a year later and dragged the *Enquirer* into the biggest embarrassment in local media history—front-page retractions and a $14 million settlement. Behind that portentous "however" was an impressive investigation that seemed to be carefully designed to support the assumption that the police were guilty. As far as the cops were concerned, the minds of reporters and editors were made up before they made their first phone call, and the headline was written before the story: "Misuse of force."

The police figured out where the reporters were going with the story and refused to cooperate. After it was published, police union leaders and assistant chiefs scorched the *Enquirer* on talk radio.

The series reported some eye-opening news that police internal investigations had ruled an officer used excessive force only once in nearly 1,400 investigations. It said victims were not paid enough for their injuries, and that even when cops failed to report using force, they were not disciplined.

But then the series reached too far and blamed it all on racism. The pictures and stories made much of the fact that 70 percent of the victims were black, while most of the cops were white. But readers had to go deep into the long, multi-part series to discover an almost hidden disclaimer:

"Although the figures mirror those of Cincinnati's annual arrest rates—in which about 70 percent of those arrested are African-American—they nonetheless underscore a long-held and growing perception in the city's black community that the city's predominantly white police force frequently mistreats African-Americans."

There was no evidence of any pattern of racism. Only "a widespread and growing perception" that was evidently shared by the reporters—who made it more "widespread and growing" by treating speculation as fact.

If the incidence of force matched arrest rates by race, there was in fact no data to substantiate such claims of racism. But the story nonetheless said the statistics "underscored" a "perception" that blacks were mistreated. And to back it up, the story quoted local NAACP leader Milton Hinton, who readily reached for a conclusion that the story did not support.

"That which we knew . . . is now substantiated by the data," said Hinton.

It also quoted an expert from Washington, D.C., who brought in just the image guaranteed to "underline growing perceptions," even if the perception was unfair. "People still remember Police Commissioner Bull Connor unleashing dogs on African-Americans to quell civil unrest in Birmingham, Ala., in 1963," the expert said in the story. "Images of police turning fire hoses on African-Americans also remain in people's memories . . . And the decades are full of examples of African-Americans being arrested, beaten and jailed falsely."

Although many blacks in Cincinnati supported the police, their voices were drowned out by unsupported accusations of racism and brutality. A witness of one alleged incident was quoted, "People don't understand why (African-Americans) are afraid of police. This is why we are afraid. In our neighborhoods, we need the police . . . to be on our side. But in our neighborhoods, we say, 'Why call the police?' We all know that police brutality is an everyday thing here."

The story won the reporters, John Hopkins and Mark Braykovich, a prestigious Best of Gannett First Place Award for investigative reporting. It was one of the first award winners for Beaupre in his effort to publish a new hard-hitting *Enquirer*, before his effort to win a Pulitzer Prize blew up in Chiquita disgrace in 1998, and he was replaced by Ward Bushee.

And seen now from a distance, "Misuse of Force" became yeast in the dough that eventually rose and swelled to become "15 black men murdered by police" in national news stories and local protests during the riots in 2001.

But it was not until race riots had already erupted that the *Enquirer* finally set the record straight. The cops were right: the truth was not so sensational.

In the late 1990s, police shootings of black men suddenly escalated along with rising crime. For three years in a row, from 1998 to 2000, police killed three men per year, far lower than other cities of similar size. Then in the year of the riots, 2001, five were killed. A study done by councilman David Pepper in 2004 showed that even those numbers were below average for a city the size of Cincinnati. But by reaching all the way back to 1995, it was true that 15 black men were killed by police in five years.

Describing the deaths "in custody" was not only wrong, but made them sound as if all the men were killed in jail, in handcuffs or sitting in police cruisers. The real story of the 15 was nothing like that. Most were violently resisting arrest, willing to fight or shoot the police to AVOID custody, or they would not have been shot.

Here are the "15 black men":

1. **Harvey Price** brutally raped a 15-year-old girl in 1995, beheaded her with an axe and held off police for four hours, attacking them with a steak knife after being hit repeatedly with mace and stun guns. He was shot when he lunged at the police with the knife.

2. **Darryll Price** (no relation) stopped traffic in 1996, jumped on the hood of a car and shouted that he was going to "shoot someone." Police sprayed mace in his face and he fell, hitting his head on the ground. The cops put him in handcuffs and called an ambulance, but Price died of "agitated delirium with restraint," an autopsy showed— usually caused by drug abuse and/or mental illness.

3. **Jermaine Lowe** was a parole violator, wanted for armed robbery when he led police on a car chase in 1998, hit another car and emptied his handgun at police. The police returned fire and killed him.

4. **Daniel Williams** flagged down Cincinnati Police officer Kathleen Conway in 1998, slugged her in the face and shot her four times in the legs and abdomen with a .357 magnum while trying to carjack her police cruiser. He had previous convictions for domestic violence and felonious assault. In self-defense, Lieutenant Conway shot him twice in the head. Conway was awarded honors for valor.

5. **Randy Black** robbed a credit union in 1998 near the University of Cincinnati campus with a handgun, and then threw a brick at cops who were chasing him. When he was cornered, he picked up a board studded with nails and lunged at a cop who shot him.

6. **James King** fired a shot while robbing a bank in 1999, threatened to take hostages and kill them and then led police on a chase through a construction site. He finally jumped out of his car, refused to drop his gun and was shot.

7. **Carey Tompkins** wrestled over a gun with a cop in the West End in 1999 as the police responded to a 911 domestic violence call at his girlfriend's apartment. Known as "C-Murda" to friends, he was shot and killed in the struggle.

8. **Alfred Pope** had 18 felony charges and five convictions by age 23 when he robbed and pistol-whipped several people in Bond Hill in 2000. When police arrived, he pulled a gun, pointed it at himself, then aimed it at the police and was shot.

9. **Jeffrey Irons** shoplifted from an Over-the-Rhine Kroger in 2000, and then fought with police as they tried to arrest him. The homeless man wrestled a gun away from a cop, shot him in the hand and was shot and killed by a second cop.

10. **Adam Wheeler** was fresh out of prison in 2001, wanted on three felony warrants when he had a shootout with the police, screaming, "You want a war? You got a war." He fired six times at the police. They shot back and killed him.

11. **Courtney Mathis**, a 12-year-old boy, took his parents' car out for a joyride. Black officer Kevin Crayon spotted him at a convenience store and reached in the car to grab the keys to stop him. Mathis hit the gas and dragged the desperate cop to death. He was shot by the dying cop; a pre-teen included in the "15 black men murdered by police."

12. **Lorenzo Collins**, a drug abuser and mental patient, escaped from a hospital in 1997 and threatened police with a brick. When he lunged at them, two officers opened fire and killed him.

13. **Michael Carpenter** tried to drive away while a cop reached into his car to take his keys in 1999. He bounced his vehicle off a parked car and was shot by the cop's partner.

14. **Roger Owensby Jr.** fought with police outside a convenience store and resisted arrest on outstanding warrants in 2000. After a violent struggle he was finally cuffed and put in the back of a police cruiser, where he died of asphyxiation.

15. **Timothy Thomas** resisted arrest and fled in 2001. He was shot as he came around a corner in a dark alley.

The "war" in the streets had casualties on both sides. Cops who were killed, like Officer Crayon, were seldom mentioned in stories about claims of "15 black men killed by police."

On Dec. 5, 1997, Officers Daniel Pope, 35, and Ronald Jeter, 34, were working the late shift when they went to serve a domestic violence warrant on Alonzo Davenport, who had several warrants out for his arrest on charges of drug abuse, speeding and passing bad checks. As they entered Davenport's Clifton Heights apartment, he pulled a gun from his pants and shot both officers before they could draw their guns. He ran a few blocks, and then witnesses saw him turn the .38 on himself and commit suicide. Pope was white, Jeter was black.

At Pope's funeral, Father James Bramlage at historic St. Peter in Chains Cathedral next door to City Hall urged the city to unite in peace to respect and thank the police. "These are the people who guard the common safety and in doing that put their lives on the line every day," he said.

Ultimately, only four of the "15 black men killed by police" were questionable. And three of those four were ruled justifiable. Critics of the Lorenzo Collins shooting said the circle of cops who surrounded him in a backyard could have found another way to stop him. But even spelling "if only" takes longer than the split-second those cops had to choose between deadly force or taking a lethal brick in the head. The city settled a racial profiling lawsuit by paying $200,000 to Collins' family. But an FBI and Justice Department investigation exonerated the officers.

Critics of the Michael Carpenter shooting said the cop never should have reached in to become tangled in the steering wheel. Stories reported that Carpenter was unarmed—which is true unless a car counts as a deadly weapon. Investigations by the Department of Justice, the county prosecutor and the Cincinnati Police exonerated the cop who fired the shots. A citizens' review panel said the shooting was unjustified. One cop resigned; the other was ordered to take additional training.

The two officers who arrested Roger Owensby were prosecuted for going over the line and accused of applying a killing choke-hold; juries acquitted both.

"The average citizen expects us to take care of those situations, and sometimes it isn't pretty," FOP President Keith Fangman told the *Enquirer*, responding to threats of violent protests over the verdict. "Police officers deal with the worst elements of society, violent individuals who violently resist arrest."

This leaves only Timothy Thomas, whose death set off the riots. He was unarmed, but ran to evade arrest. "That was an unintentional discharge of a firearm," said Lieutenant Colonel Richard Janke. "It was not an appropriate shooting."

At the scene, witnesses said the officer who shot Thomas, Stephen Roach, said "it just went off." Later, he said he saw Thomas reaching into his pants and thought he might have a weapon.

Cincinnati was torn apart. Half the city said Roach was lying and changed his story to cover up an accidental or even deliberate shooting. The other half said if Roach thought Thomas had a gun, it was justified.

Fangman was president of the police union at the time. He says there's another possibility.

"There were 17 police-shooting deaths during my tenure, so I had a pretty good idea of how it was supposed to go," Keith Fangman said. "But the minute I walked into the interrogation room and took one look at Steve Roach, by the look on his face I knew this was going to be a problem. He had his head in his hands. I asked, 'Steve, are you OK?' He just shook his head no.'"

The story circulated through the city that Roach changed his story after talking to his FOP lawyer. Fangman insists that didn't happen. "I have no doubt that Timothy Thomas was reaching down to pull up his pants. They came around the corner at the same moment and nearly ran into each other. Roach had his finger on the trigger and, bam, it startled Roach and he fired the shot. I believe both are true. Roach was startled and the gun went off, and Thomas was coming around the corner, pulling up his pants."

Judge Ted Winkler, presiding at Roach's trial, found Roach not guilty. But the police internal investigation found Roach was wrong and Police Chief Tom Streicher concluded that the officer lied and was not fit to work for Cincinnati. By then, Roach had already resigned and moved on.

One in 15 was wrong, according to lengthy investigations. Among the 15 cases, only Owensby and Darryll Price were "in custody" when they died.

Two—Owensby and Carpenter—were questionable because of mistakes in police procedure that may have caused or contributed to their deaths.

City Journal writer Heather MacDonald, who visited Cincinnati to cover the riots and their aftermath, reported that statistics proved a Cincinnati police officer was 27 times more likely to be killed by a black man, than a black man was likely to be killed by a Cincinnati cop. The odds of black men killed by black men are off the charts.

But by the time the complete story finally came out, the city was already in chaos. The myth of "15 black men" was everywhere and complaints from the relatives of the dead men fueled the "widespread and growing perception" of a police department that was "hunting down young black men," as rioters claimed.

Police overreacted, said the aunt of Harvey Price, the man who raped and beheaded Tesha Beasley. "It just seems like when white men commit a crime, they still end up with their day in court," she told the *Enquirer*. "All 15 of those men killed by police were black, and that's the problem that has caused all of this."

That could almost be a summary of the Misuse of Force series. Black men who caused a disproportionate share of violent crime were more likely to be injured in arrests—but because they were black, the police must be racist.

÷÷÷

Lieutenant Colonel Janke objected that the statistics in Misuse of Force were irrelevant and misleading unless they could be put in the context of crime. Was crime going up? Yes. Does rising crime mean more use of force? Yes. If blacks make up a disproportionate share of crime, will they also be make up a disproportionate share of use-of-force reports? Yes again.

Even 1,400 reports "was a very small database," said Janke. "What about all the arrests without using force? You have to compare it to that, and to how many resisted arrest, how many ran, and how much violent crime you have. If violent crime is up, use of force is up."

A year after the riots, a more scientific study was conducted by the University of Cincinnati to find out if the Cincinnati Police were using racial profiling. The UC researchers took many of the variables mentioned by Janke into account, and found that there was no evidence of profiling. Blacks were arrested more often because they accounted for a disproportionate amount of crime, the report said.

In 2005, one of the most ambitious studies in the nation of race, discrimination and arrest data was conducted in Cincinnati by the Rand Corporation. Rand said its report on Cincinnati Police was the most ambitious of its kind anywhere in the country. The conclusion: no evidence of racial profiling, discrimination or unfair treatment of minorities by the Cincinnati Police Department.

"There was no difference in the type of force used against individuals of different races," said the 400-page Rand Corp. report.

Janke was right. Finding increased use of force without looking at the big picture of rising crime was like publishing an alarming story that traffic accidents had doubled—without telling readers that there were twice as many drivers on the roads.

"My main complaint was that a newspaper doesn't have the space to do this accurately," Janke said.

A letter to the editor from July, 1997, responding to the "Misuse of Force" series, expressed the way most cops felt.

Low ethical standards

The *Enquirer* has displayed a new low in ethical standards for journalism.

If the truth does not fit into your overall scheme of sensationalism and rhetoric, don't report it. If the facts don't support your biased view, distort them to fit your own agenda. In your recent articles and editorials concerning the men and women of the Cincinnati Police Division, you brought these omissions and distortions to a new low ["Misuse of force," June 22-24 and "Police respond," July 6].

As retired police officers, we take pride in our reputations and we support the current police officers of our local departments who give so much to their community. This is not a blanket support. When their actions are proven justified by the facts and proper investigations, these officers have rights, too. The reporting should not be slanted by innuendo and distortion.

Hike Bogosian
President, Association of Retired Cincinnati and Hamilton
County Police Officers

÷ ÷ ÷

During the five years leading up to the riots, from 1997 to 2001, the *Enquirer* published at least a dozen major stories that criticized the Cincinnati Police, including several major team reporting projects like "Misuse of Force." Those stories won numerous journalism awards—judged by other journalists, from outside Cincinnati.

For example, the Society for Professional Journalists gave a 2003 story second place, and a judge said it was "A stellar use of FOIA to illustrate epidemic racism in the police department."

Contest-winning headlines included: "Police Brutality" (about the arrest of Pharon Crosby); "Racial Profiling," "Police Review Themselves," "With Guns Drawn" and "Police Discipline Unequal: records show blacks get more punishment" (later contradicted by "Discipline Report Inconclusive"). The stories accused the Cincinnati Police of racism, profiling, brutality, misuse of force, covering up complaints, bigotry against black officers and bribery (never substantiated).

Other local media often echoed the same theme established by the city's dominant morning paper. No institution in Cincinnati—no business, government, schools or social or political issues—was put in such a harsh spotlight of relentless scrutiny and criticism. Cops believe the media were on a crusade to prove that the Cincinnati Police Division was a cesspool of corruption, reeking with racism.

They still wonder why.

As criticism of media bias has increased in recent years, studies have repeatedly shown that journalists' attitudes and voting patterns are far more liberal than most of the readers and communities they serve.

Part of the anti-police attitude may be a clash of cultures. Journalism tends to attract people who want to change the world, help the poor, fight injustice and question authority.

Most reporters and editors are ingrained or trained with a mistrust of authority. And cops represent the blunt edge of authority in society.

During the 1990s, the Rodney King story reinforced that mistrust. Journalists are herd animals, and the King beating video became the template for similar stories in cities nationwide, wherever ugly but necessary use of force by police was caught on tape or witnessed by shocked citizens and reporters.

The feeling of mistrust is mutual. Many cops don't like or trust journalists—for pretty good reasons—and operate in their own tight-knit, exclusive tribe behind the invisible blue line. That sets off alarm bells and suspicion in newsrooms.

And during the 1990s and early 2000s, the media was infected by a contagious form of cultural cowardice called political correctness. In an effort to be more inclusive and promote diversity, newsrooms often gave blank checks to minority reporters and their viewpoints, as if they were beyond the routine rules of challenge, verification and editorial skepticism.

Most Cincinnati and national media followed the same P.C. script in riot coverage, playing the story as a "rebellion" against racist police, or at least "unrest" over root causes such as poverty, lack of jobs, welfare cuts and inadequate schools, usually leaving out the explanation that seemed obvious to cops, that it was violence and lawlessness for its own sake, with no hidden message or justification.

Former Assistant Police Chief Rick Biehl remembers an interview during riot week with a reporter from the *New York Times*.

"It was the day of the Timothy Thomas funeral. He was asking all the right questions. I spoke with him for half an hour on the phone. I told him it was enormously misleading to keep repeating the line about fifteen black men killed in custody. I explained about the need for context, and went through all those cases with him.

"Then when I read the *Times* the next day I was ready to puke. When it came out there were only two or three lines from our entire conversation."

And the myth of the 15 black men was repeated again—without any context or explanation.

Mayor Charlie Luken remembers the same frustration with local media. He singled out the *Enquirer* because it had the most local influence. "The coverage of the entire events during the riots fostered more rioting and problems," he said. He complained to editors and reporters, he said. "They told me there was an agenda."

Assistant Managing Editor at the time Rick Green denies it. "We had no agenda but to cover the news," he said.

Luken, a former TV newsman, said he took his objections to the publisher. "I told Harry Whipple, 'You guys are trying to win a Pulitzer at the expense of your city.' I still believe it's true. They entered the riot coverage for a Pulitzer and they probably would have even won if not for 9-11 that year, because the Pulitzer judges don't know the truth."

In most respects, the *Enquirer's* coverage of the riots was outstanding. Reporters and photographers risked their own safety to wade into the violence and get the stories. Many in the local media, at the *Cincinnati Post* and radio and TV stations, distinguished themselves.

The *Enquirer* won first place in Best of Gannett for its riot coverage, including a photo essay titled "Rebellion."

Luken says he told Whipple, "Look at the way the *Enquirer* treats a story when a police officer is involved in a shooting. You put his picture in the paper like a mug shot, and bring up every miscue and complaint against him in his entire career."

By comparison, riot and boycott leader the Rev. Damon Lynch III of the Black United Front was treated on an equal footing with the elected mayor of the city throughout the riots and the aftermath, without the same scrutiny, Luken said. "If Damon Lynch caught a cold, someone from the *Enquirer* would call to ask me why I made him sick."

"Who the hell elected him to anything?" Luken wondered. "Anything I said got a response quote from Damon and everything he said deserved a comment from me."

"They put the story announcing Lynch's boycott on Page One on

Sunday. If you put that on the front page on a Sunday in any city, they're going to have problems."

For a year after the riots, Lynch was not challenged by the local or national media to provide names or the number of members in his Black United Front, although he represented the group in a class action lawsuit against the city. His own background and credibility, including his role in triggering the riots, escaped scrutiny. He was treated with an uncharacteristic lack of skepticism—as if the normal rules had been suspended.

Finally, a year after the riots, a few big advertisers, representing car dealerships, hotels, real estate companies and developer Neil Bortz, sat down with Whipple in the 20th-floor boardroom at the Enquirer and delivered a boycott threat of their own: stop splashing Lynch and his boycott all over the newspaper, or else.

"We told him, 'You're killing our city,'" Bortz said. "The city was taking a beating from the front page to the editorial page. In every story, Damon Lynch was the hero.

"We were not threatening anything, but we just wanted to get the news reported evenly. What finally did it was they had run a story in which they called some of the leaders of the Black United Front 'community activists,' with nothing about their backgrounds or their police records. Then they ran a profile of the cops who had the most complaints and it had everything including their high school and the number of kids they had."

"We just wanted to let him know that a lot of people who were using his media for advertising were not happy about it."

Whipple, a fierce defender of the newsroom, who was not the kind to back down to pressure from advertisers, walked out of the meeting, Bortz said.

But gradually, the Damon Lynch free publicity tour on the front pages came to an end.

For a year, the local media handed the biggest media megaphone in town to Lynch, filling his scrapbook with boycott publicity clippings and headlines, which he used to encourage entertainers and speakers to snub Cincinnati, tarnish the city's reputation and choke tourist business for restaurants, hotels and downtown businesses.

In a December 2001 letter, Lynch wrote:

> "Police are killing, raping, planting false evidence, and along with the Prosecutor and courts are destroying the general sense of self-respect for black citizens.
> "IF YOUR ORGANIZATION IS PLANNING AN EVENT IN CINCINNATI, OR IF YOU ARE PLANNING TO ATTEND AN EVENT HERE, PLEASE CANCEL."

Cincinnati police officers believe Misuse of Force and other stories like it laid the foundation for Lynch's wild claims that Cincinnati Police were rapists and murderers. They say uncritical coverage of him after the riots filled his boycott tank with free headlines that aggravated the damage to Cincinnati.

So was the coverage award-winning journalism, or as the cops claimed, contest journalism run amok?

The quality and comprehensiveness of the newspaper stories is outstanding. But there is also no question that the boycotters found it sympathetic. From March 1 to April 29 in 2002, the *Enquirer* (40) and *Post* (17) ran 57 boycott stories that were posted on the boycotters' web site— not including even more sympathetic support from the alternative weekly *CityBeat*.

Like "Misuse of Force," the boycott was a legitimate, important story for the region. But 57 boycott stories in less than two months is almost one every day.

"I told Whipple, 'Put an asterisk by the boycott in your headlines,'" Luken said. "It should say, 'Brought to you by *The Cincinnati Enquirer*.'"

Rioters vaulted a fence to flee on April 10 as police fired beanbag shotguns in a confrontation on Central Parkway near the Kroger Building.

CHAPTER 9

RIOT HISTORY 101

April is the cruelest month, breeding
Lilacs out of the dead land, mixing
Memory and desire, stirring
Dull roots with spring rain.

— *T.S. Eliot, "The Wasteland"*

April is a pretty cruel month for riots, too. For some reason—spring fever outbreaks or an accident of history—some of the worst riots in history have erupted in April.

The year 1968, at the peak of the civil rights movement, goes down as the worst year for contagious riots in America. Forty-six people were killed and 7,000 were injured in 130 cities including Chicago, Baltimore, Washington, Newark and Cincinnati. That same year, riots, strikes, sit-ins and protests disturbed the peace on 300 college campuses. Images of the riots at the 1968 Democratic National Convention in Chicago have become the TV shorthand for our national memory of the police vs. protesters clashes of the "the 60s."

Even in high schools, 60 percent had protests, sit-ins or student strikes in 1968, according to the book "Riots U.S.A." by Willard A. Heaps.

And it all began in April that year, with the assassination of Martin Luther King on April 4, 1968. "Grief and anger" turned into "organized orgies of arson and thievery," Heaps wrote.

With a court verdict on April 29, 1991, the Rodney King riots set South Central Los Angeles ablaze like an urban bonfire. When those riots ended, 51 people were killed and 2,383 were injured.

Ten years later, on April 9, 2001, riots came again in Cincinnati. They were the worst riots since L.A., and they grabbed national and international attention for a week. Cincinnati, the placid, peaceful, safe and family friendly Queen City of the Midwest, the historic home of the Underground Railroad, was suddenly ground zero in America's race conflict. A city that symbolized heartland values was ripped apart by the kind of race-riot earthquake most Americans expected to see only on the fringes of civic sanity, in edgy mega-cities such as Los Angeles or Detroit.

What happened in Cincinnati looked a lot like a smaller, made-for-TV version of the epic big-screen riots in Los Angeles. Both were more than just riots. They were race riots: lawless violence, arson and looting by blacks who targeted police and whites.

But the aftermath in Cincinnati may eventually have a lot more in common with the 1967 riots that left Detroit a hollowed-out husk, a city still comatose, kept alive by state-revenue feeding tubes nearly 40 years later.

The ugly scars of that Detroit riot are still showing. Population flight. Epidemic crime. Corrupt and incompetent political leadership. Imploding finances. Detroit has become a long-term care patient, kept alive by huge transfusions of state and federal aid, a decaying symbol of what cities like Cincinnati desperately hope to avoid.

It's hard to believe now, but in the early 1960s Detroit was considered a model city. Then, in the summer of 1967 Detroit became the monster in Michigan's nightmares. Even in sleepy little towns like Corunna, the Mayberry-style seat of Shiawassee County, 90 miles and two hours northwest of Detroit, men gathered at the Elks Club, the VFW and the Masonic Temple and talked over cans of Schlitz and Pabst about arming themselves so they would be ready for the uprising that was sure to follow the burning of Detroit—as if fear was spread like a plume of radioactive fallout from the smoke over the Motor City.

After that summer, Detroit was no longer the bustling metropolis of Michigan's future. It became a city of fear and crime, a shameful symbol of failure and hate.

In March of 1968, a commission appointed by President Lyndon Johnson visited riot-torn cities, studied the problems, and reported, "The white majority is essentially to blame for the situation." Johnson did his best to ignore the embarrassing report. The next president, Richard Nixon, was more direct. He said the report "blames everybody for the riots except the perpetrators."

More than 30 years later, history repeated. Cincinnati had the same reaction: appoint a commission, blame white society, then ignore the find-ings and argue about it, waiting for someone who is honest and brave enough to point out that riots are caused by rioters.

It's an old debate—as old as riots in America, which have a colorful and fascinating history that has been enthusiastically ignored, swept away in a hurry along with all the broken glass.

Americans have rioted over stamps, taxes, whiskey, and religion. They've rioted and murdered each other over immigration, the draft, wages and working conditions. They've even rioted over body-snatching doctors, versions of the Bible, and an actor who was too British.

÷ ÷ ÷

Probably the first major riot documented in America happened in Boston in 1765, when hundreds of colonists protested British Stamp Act taxes by destroying a building, breaking windows and burning furniture. It was that riot that spawned the famous rallying cry, "No taxation without represen-tation." And it was led, in part, by rabble-rousing American patriots John Hancock and Samuel Adams. The violence was finally subdued when troops were called out to literally read the Riot Act, a British law dating from 1715. The Riot Act gave rioters one hour to disperse or be arrested for a felony. It worked.

In 1788, New York City, a town of 25,000 at the time, grabbed a place in riot history for the most bizarre and gruesome riot: the Doctors Riot. Anger was growing over body-snatcher medical students who plundered fresh graves for cadavers to dissect and study. The riots were sparked when a medical student waved a severed arm in the face of a window-peeping boy and told him "This is your mother," according to historical accounts. The boy's outraged father, who had lost his wife just weeks before, the leg-end goes, went to the cemetery and found her body was stolen. A mob formed and stormed the medical school and local hospital. This time, fa-mous American patriots—John Jay and Alexander Hamilton—were on the other side of the rock-throwing riots, and both were stoned only weeks after finishing the Federalist Papers that were supposed to be a blueprint for a civil society. Eight people were killed, including three soldiers. Mayor James Duane was trampled, but vowed nonetheless to punish the grave robbers.

There were anti-Catholic riots in Philadelphia in 1844—mainly aimed at Irish immigrants who had demanded a Catholic version for mandatory Bible study in schools. Two dozen were killed, more than 100 were wounded, and the riots spread to other cities with large immigrant populations.

An arrogant British actor who became a scapegoat for anti-English resentment was pelted with pennies, lemons, apples, old shoes, "eggs of doubtful purity" and potatoes, setting off the Astor Place Riots in New York City in 1849. Cannons were used to clear the streets.

Thirty-one were killed, 40 wounded.

There were anti-Chinese riots in Los Angeles in 1871, steelworker riots in Homestead, Penn. in 1892, railroad worker riots in Chicago in 1894, and miner riots in Coeur d'Alene, Idaho in 1899.

The deadliest riots in American history broke out during the Civil War in New York City. During the Draft Riots of 1863, a mob of 70,000 looted, burned, lynched and murdered for four days to protest draft rules that allowed wealthy draftees to dodge the war by paying $300 to send a poorer man instead. A gun factory was attacked in a deadly battle with police and 2,000 guns were stolen. And the rioters turned their senseless wrath on blacks, who were blamed for the war. The ensuing race riot was a bloodbath, stopped finally with howitzers. The death toll was estimated at from 500 to 1,000.

"Ugliest Riot" award goes to East St. Louis, where the local paper trumpeted a headline in 1917: "100 Negroes Shot, Burned and Clubbed to Death."

There were Zoot Suit riots in L.A. in 1943, targeting Mexicans and blacks. A race riot in Detroit the same year killed 34, and was blamed on the weakness of the police.

Not including prison riots and dozens of smaller riots in surprisingly small towns like Evansville, Ind., America has had riots almost as regularly as elections.

But the Watts riots in 1965 shocked the nation and set a new modern benchmark, with 34 killed and more than 1,000 injured in six days of race riots that choked the city of Los Angeles in a blanket of acrid smoke and eye-stinging hatred.

The following year, riots broke out in eight cities. The year after that, 1967, there were 123 minor riots, 33 serious riots and major riots in Cincinnati, Tampa, Boston, Chicago, Atlanta, Dayton and Detroit, where

Sherman tanks, halftracks and helicopters used .50 caliber machine guns to blast snipers on rooftops. For a week in July, Detroit was occupied by more than 13,000 U.S. Army troops.

Michigan was terrorized from Corunna to the Mackinaw Bridge. In many ways, Americans never got over it. Neither did Detroit.

And as different as all those riots were in causes and casualties, there are common threads of stupidity and madness that tie most of them together.

Politics: From the start, political leaders can incite and aggravate riots, like John Hancock and Sam Adams—or get stoned for opposing them like John Jay and Alexander Hamilton.

In Los Angeles, in 1991, Mayor Tom Bradley tacitly endorsed violence by calling the police officers who were found not guilty in the Rodney King trial "renegade cops." When the verdict came out, rather than try to educate and calm the public, he said, "No explanation makes sense."

The wrong or reckless initial reaction by political leaders and the media are critical in setting a tone of justification and "permission" to riot. In Cincinnati, political leaders on City Council aggravated and incited violence by appeasing protesters and siding with them against the police.

Racism: Dozens of deadly race riots swept the country in the early 1900s and again in the 1940s, caused by white racism against minorities, especially blacks. Since the 1960s, the coin has flipped and modern race riots are driven by blacks who attack whites—usually "justified" by incendiary accusations of white bigotry and oppression. In Detroit and Watts, the excuse was discrimination and poverty. In Los Angeles and Cincinnati, it was police brutality and profiling. But when blacks single out innocent whites, drag them from their cars and beat them, that is still ignorant, hateful racism.

Show of force: In every riot, an immediate, overwhelming show of force can be critical to avoid violence. Every lost minute, hour and day of delay raises the stakes and multiplies the mayhem. The Hall of Shame nominee for weakness under pressure is Columbia University President

Grayson Kirk, who refused to call in New York City Police for six days while thousands of students occupied his administration building and took college officials hostage in 1968.

In his book *Fires and Furies: The L.A. Riots,* James Delk writes about the initial outbreak in 1991 at the intersection of Florence and Normandie: "In a highly controversial decision, the police retreated from the scene rather than being reinforced. Later there were several explanations for pulling out. One was that there were not enough police officers and they were poorly equipped for a riot. Another was the conviction that police were the targets of anger, so removing the targets should defuse the crowd's anger. This was the same rationale that was often used to explain actions that led up to the Watts riot, and didn't work any better this time than it did back then."

Ten years later, Cincinnati City Council kept cops out of a council meeting that spawned the riots, because some council members feared the presence of cops in uniform would antagonize the crowd of blacks protesting a police shooting of a fleeing suspect. As Delk said, "Pulling police out seemed to merely embolden the rioters."

A strong and early show of force can prevent violence. The Riot Act worked in the first American riots. Cincinnati discovered that the modern version, a curfew, worked in 2001.

Blame: After the Irish churches and schools were burned in Boston in 1844, Philadelphia decided to blame the primary victims—Irish Catholics—for the riots. In 1871, California decided to blame the Chinese who were lynched by a mob shouting "Burn the Chinks." And even the trampled mayor of New York City quickly moved to appease the mob and blame the medical student victims for the Doctor's Riot of 1788.

More recently, the Los Angeles Police were blamed for the 1991 Rodney King riots. And in Cincinnati, the police were blamed for the race riots of 2001, although they never fired a shot of live ammunition and, amazingly, nobody was killed.

Agitators: Even "spontaneous" riots usually have a hothead or calculating "igniter" who incites the crowd with passion or pushes a cold-blooded political or union cause. It was revolutionary patriots in the 1765;

then it was anti-war, anti-Lincoln Democrats and Confederate sympathizers in the draft riots of 1863. It was union leaders or corporate union-busting goons in the early 1900s; and in the 1960s it was black militants and SDS student radicals.

But in the latest major riots, something new has happened. Suddenly, the media are playing a largely overlooked role as agitator and inciter.

During the arrest of Rodney King, a man on a nearby balcony filmed the incident on a video camera. He recorded more than 80 seconds of tape—but the media only showed the most inflammatory 30 seconds showing King being beaten with batons while he was on the ground. The part of the tape that showed King lunging at the cops, even after being stunned by Tasers twice, was not shown.

That missing tape "explains why the jurors in the pro-police, conservative community of Simi Valley ruled the way they did," wrote Lou Cannon in his book, *Official Negligence: How Rodney King and the Riots Changed Los Angeles and the LAPD.*

"They thought that the media hadn't told them the full story, and lo and behold, we hadn't. But in trials, if there is evidence that is damaging to your side, it's going to come out one way or the other. So lawyers try to present it, to give their own spin on it before the other side can present it. As the King trial begins, the prosecutor, who is an African-American, Terry White, a very fine lawyer, is giving the opening statement. He is showing the jury this unedited tape. Their mouths are agape. They are saying the mental equivalent of 'ah-ha.' So, in his opening statement, White has to explain away part of the tape, and to describe King as the person who was hostile. That wasn't the only problem with the trial. King didn't testify, the prosecution had poor witnesses, the other side had good witnesses. But the prosecution really never recovered from the videotape."

L.A. Police Chief Daryl Gates said on ABC's "Nightline," "Expectations of a guilty verdict were brought on by the electronic media and the print media. The electronic media kept playing that thing over and over and over and kept saying how terrible it was."

That tape was played nationally and in Cincinnati, setting up expectations that police routinely brutalize black suspects and get away with it; that any rough arrest caught on tape is "another Rodney

King"; that similar stories were happening in cities everywhere, and it was the media's job to find them and expose the corrupt, racist police.

In Cincinnati, the media took the popular expectations another step closer to the ragged edge of mob violence—picking up where the King tape left off. Videotape of a rough takedown of a black high school student who resisted arrest was shown repeatedly on local TV news in 1997—ratifying the distorted image of "another Rodney King." A series of print investigative stories portrayed the police as rogues and renegades, reinforcing the black community's "barbershop history" of cops as brutal racists and bigots.

Meanwhile, the loudest agitator and his Black United Front were given a free pass by the local media. The race riots were reported as a "rebellion" or "unrest"—semantically endorsing an excuse for inexcusable violence. And after the riots, the local media continued to agitate by giving generous headline coverage to the Black United Front boycott of Cincinnati.

What nearly all of these deadly outbreaks of lawlessness, hatred and violence often have in common is the Four Rs:

Rumors agitate and inflame a crowd;

Rock throwing signals the onset of mob madness;

Rapid response by police is critical to show swift and overwhelming force, or the next step is:

Riots.

Couch-burning crowds of alcohol-fueled college students can be classified as a "riot," but they don't compare in size, intensity or ugliness to the race riots that rocked a once-peaceful city in middle America. Although both are dangerous, college "riots" and race riots are as different in scale as shoplifting and armed robbery.

What happened in Cincinnati can happen in nearly every American city. The Cincinnati riots are one more chapter in the darkest pages of American history—mistakes, miracles, blunders, bold decisions, good guys and bad guys, racism and racial reconciliation.

The media version has played over and over, like a Rodney King tape-loop of "root causes," "unrest" and "rebellion."

But there's another, untold story of what really happened in Cincinnati in April 2001.

It doesn't fit the media script at all.

Police on horseback and in riot gear formed
a line in front of Police Headquarters on
the evening of April 9 as the crowd of
protesters swelled to more than 1,000 and
began throwing rocks and bottles.

CHAPTER 10

A STATE
FUNERAL

T he relics of Cincinnati's faith are scattered throughout the city. The old downtown churches stand out like hand-carved antiques in a mass-produced modern world. Although they stand in the shadows of streamlined, towering office buildings of glass and steel, they somehow manage to give the impression that they reach higher in a cascade of ornate stonework, spires, and bell towers and arched stained-glass windows that point to the heavens.

The treasured old churches survive almost untouched, reminders of a different time, like wooden ships of architecture berthed in a marina of modern fiberglass and steel luxury yachts.

New Prospect Baptist Church in Over-the-Rhine doesn't belong in either harbor. It has no towers, spires or crosses thrust toward the clouds. It squats like a large convenience store or small brick post office, flat, square and brown. At the back is a narrow cobblestone street, lined with old buildings of peeling red-painted bricks. Weathered boards cover some windows, while others are dark, deep and empty as a dead man's eyes.

Across from the entrance of New Prospect at Findlay and Elm, historic Findlay Market is tucked behind a row of skinny, four-story old shops and apartments, where more boarded windows have narrow openings like gun slits.

A sign in front of the church shows a lamb and lion lying down together, and quotes from the scripture, which is partially covered by splashed paint. Nothing in Over-the-Rhine, not even the sacred church of the celebrated protester-peacemaker The Rev. Damon Lynch III, is safe from vandalism, bullet holes and the disfiguring scars of random, senseless destruction.

But this unlikely, homely little church, deep in the war zone of looting, arson, beatings and gunfire, was where rioters, reverends, politicians and preachers all gathered to pray for peace on Saturday, April 14, at the funeral of Timothy Thomas.

Thomas, an unemployed 19-year-old who left behind a child, fit the standard description of nearly all the young black men who were killed in Over-the-Rhine. "He was just about to turn his life around," they always say. Police acknowledge there is no proof he was involved in the drug trade, but he was killed on the streets in a time and place that is almost exclusive territory of drug dealers and their customers. He had 14 warrants for his arrest: three for driving with an expired driver's license, four for seat belt violations, five for driving with no driver's license and two for obstruction of official business.

He was dreaming of a career in electronics if he could first get a high-school diploma, the news stories reported next to his picture in a tuxedo. He was one of six children raised by a single mother who had moved her family from Chicago to Cincinnati a few years earlier. On paper, he was interchangeable with thousands of anonymous young black men.

Yet when Thomas died, 500 people squeezed into the little church on Elm Street, including nearly all of Cincinnati City Council, the mayor of Cincinnati, NAACP leader Kweise Mfume, the son of Martin Luther King Jr., and Ohio Gov. Bob Taft and his wife, Hope.

The Rev. Lynch officiated.

"You could have cut the tension with a knife," said Councilman Jim Tarbell. "Taft shouldn't have been there."

The governor seemed awkward, nervous and uncomfortable, as his office and the governor himself were subjected to Lynch's emotional sermon that emphasized all the alleged root causes of riots, but offered little about Thomas. Tarbell recalled, "It just didn't seem appropriate for the governor to put himself in that position."

Lynch ended the funeral service by telling the crowd, "There are young people out there who need you. As you leave here today, do not leave posturing. Leave here hugging somebody."

But during his message, Mayor Charlie Luken said, "We were all surprised at some of the more hateful rhetoric coming from the pulpit."

According to a legend in the police division, confirmed by several officers, an aide to the mayor had called a high-ranking commander to ask for a police escort for council members who wanted to attend the funeral.

But there was a stipulation: the council members would not ride in marked police cars and wanted protection only from officers in plainclothes, no uniforms allowed.

Still furious at being blamed for riots that the cops were risking their lives to stop, his patience worn thin by 16-hour days of flying rocks and bullets, an assistant chief responded: "Why don't you call the sanitation department. They have plenty of unmarked vehicles that would be suitable."

Luken said he doesn't remember anything like that, but he says he has always wondered if the police who were sent to pick up council members after the funeral were intentionally late.

"There were a thousand or two thousand angry people in the street. As we came out, there was this long line of Chevy Suburbans, security cars for the governor and his entourage, between us and the crowd. Out comes Taft, gets in his Suburban and leaves—and then there we were, face-to-face with thousands of angry people."

Luken says several black pastors formed a protective circle around him to shield him from the crowd.

Jim Tarbell just stepped into the crowd like a man crossing an empty street on his lunch hour. Almost miraculously, the crowd parted for Tarbell and the tension was broken.

On rooftops and hidden in an unmarked van nearby, police SWAT teams and snipers heaved a sigh of relief. They were there to protect the governor and get him out "in case his ass got kicked," said a SWAT commander.

They were ready to take a bullet for Taft if they had to. And as it turned out, some did sustain nearly fatal career wounds because of the governor's visit that day.

But the cops had no doubt Taft should not have been there. He did nothing to help the situation. His presence only aggravated problems and caused a security nightmare—the state's highest-ranking political official in a riot zone. Taft's condolences made Thomas sound like a martyr, and made the Cincinnati Police, by implication, sound like killers who had senselessly cut down a young hero in the prime of his life.

"That was the day we all lost respect for the governor," says SWAT officer John Rose. "He never once came to a police funeral. And here he was, going to this." The anger at Taft lingers, because of what happened immediately after the funeral, a few blocks away.

As Tarbell made his way through the departing funeral mourners, "I heard this woman screaming that someone had been shot."

Tarbell, a former medic, ran to the intersection of Liberty and Elm, south of the church, and found people gathering around a woman lying in an alley. "I tried to help her, but her husband, boyfriend, whatever, stepped in front of me and started telling me, 'This is terrible, the police just shot her with no warning.' And something crossed my mind. 'How terrible can this really be,' I thought, 'if his focus was on the behavior of the officers rather than the injury to his friend?' I thought, 'This may not be what it appears.'"

In news stories it quickly became the "drive-by" police shooting of two children and a teacher who were in a "peaceful crowd."

"We didn't know if it was live ammunition," Christine Jones, the Louisville teacher, told the *Enquirer.* "I wasn't sure what I was shot with. The police cars came around the corner and stopped . . . about 20-30 feet away and got out of their cars and started firing.

"There were children there and it was a totally unprovoked attack. It reminded me of a drive-by shooting. It was as if they were trying to hurt people."

A U.S. Department of Justice investigation was launched immediately, at the invitation of Mayor Charlie Luken. Some reports said police had fired on mourners as they left the funeral. Shock waves reverberated like a bomb at a peace conference, and politicians scrambled to glue together the fragile truce they had pledged in New Prospect during the funeral.

But what really happened has little resemblance to the reports at the time, or even long after.

Christine Jones came to Cincinnati all the way from Louisville that day as a member of a Louisville group, Citizens Against Police Abuse. She was there not as a teacher, but as an anti-police protester.

"She had no business being there," said one of the SWAT officers who later became known as "The Beanbag Six."

"She was blocking the street like everyone else," said Officer Tim Pappas.

According to records from an eight-month investigation by the FBI and the Department of Justice, obtained under the Freedom of Information Act, Pappas and the cops were right—and most of the news reports were misleading and unfair to the cops involved.

Two state troopers and four Cincinnati cops, called to clear an intersection to protect the governor, were presumed guilty. The troopers were almost immediately exonerated. But the Cincinnati cops were dragged through a nightmare of threats and intimidation. When they were finally cleared, the governor never even said "thank you." The investigation destroyed one cop's career and forced several to resign from the SWAT team in protest. It might even have put some innocent cops in prison if not for a battle behind the scenes that went all the way to the White House.

Before it was over, the cops were threatened with hard prison time unless they admitted criminal violations of federal civil rights laws and testified against each other. Each of them spent $7,000 to $17,000 each in legal fees, and was held in legal limbo for nearly a year.

An unidentified youth hurls a can of soda
at riot police in the middle of deserted
Race Street downtown on April 10.

CHAPTER 11

THE BEANBAG SIX

T he broken glass was swept away. Burned out and looted shops were cleaned up and reopened or closed for good. Broken windows were replaced with plywood sheets. And everywhere politicians talked and editorials pontificated, there were calls for "dialogue" and "healing."

But that's not how the rest of 2001 will be remembered. The year of the riots was also the year of "de-policing"—a slowdown by tired, angry, frustrated and fed-up Cincinnati cops.

At first, the reality of a police slowdown was adamantly denied. But the statistics said what city leaders refused to admit. Arrests dropped 30 percent—as violent crime climbed by the same percentage. By June 25, less than three months after the last fire was doused in Over-the-Rhine, shootings had gone up 600 percent from the previous year. Even routine traffic tickets fell by 50 percent.

Cops said that without political support at City Hall, their job was all pain, no gain. "Jump out" on a drug dealer selling crack on a street corner in broad daylight, and nearly all of the outcomes were a scratch on the eight-ball. The guy probably had a gun. He was likely to run, fight or do both. A cop could get killed or badly injured. And although cops were willing to take that risk, they worried about another one. Even if a cop did his job by the book, if he killed or injured a suspect his career could be destroyed by politicians who seemed to always presume suspects innocent and cops guilty.

"Why do it?" they wondered. "And if I'm not enforcing real crime in the war zone, why should I stop speeders and hand out tickets that generate revenue for the politicians who won't support us?"

Experts who study riots say this happens wherever riots give "permission" for lawlessness, and political leaders take the easy way out and blame the cops to placate loud protesters. As police morale drops, many cops see no reason to take career-killing risks or write traffic tickets for a city that betrays them in a crisis.

Or another way to explain it is to take a look at the unfair, lousy luck of Sgt. Eric Hall.

On a warm April day in 1995, a lot like the week of riots six years later, Hall was walking a beat near the Mercantile Center office building on Sixth Street and Vine in the downtown business district. Police had been getting lots of complaints from office workers and downtown visitors who had been shoved, spit on, insulted, groped or threatened by a large crowd of black teens that congregated and blocked the sidewalk at a bus stop just outside the high-rise Mercantile Center. Most of the kids were Cincinnati Public Schools students who used Metro buses to get to school. As they changed buses, the stop downtown became a favorite hangout.

On April 25, 1995, Hall approached and ordered the crowd to disperse. He quickly wound up in a physical struggle with CPS high school senior Pharon Crosby. Crosby, 18, built like a college fullback, refused Hall's orders and wrestled with the cop, tearing ligaments in Hall's shoulder. Hall called for backup and two more officers arrived. They pepper-sprayed Crosby and hit him with batons to pull him off Hall as the cop and Crosby rolled in the street. A large crowd of teens pushed in, yelling, spitting on and cursing the cops, throwing ice, cups and soft drinks. It all would have gone mostly unnoticed, but for a Channel 5 news crew that was working downtown, stumbled onto the scene, and caught the end of it on videotape.

As soon as it hit the evening news, the story was Rodney King all over again. The tape showed the physical, brutal use of force by cops trying to restrain a strong, violently resisting suspect. The tape did not include the struggle in which Crosby fought and injured Hall, only the police effort to subdue Crosby that followed.

Like the Rodney King video that ran in an endless loop on TV three years earlier, the Channel 5 tape ran over and over—showing only the most inflammatory part of the story, like watching the mushroom cloud over Hiroshima without knowing anything about Pearl Harbor.

When jurors saw the entire Rodney King tape, showing how King had attacked the cops and refused to stay down so he could be cuffed, they sided with the cops. When they learned he had led cops on a 117 mph chase, was Tasered twice and still threw off four cops before charging them, the jury acquitted the cops and the Los Angeles riots of 1991 went off like a stick of racial dynamite.

"The Rodney King videotape is true. But it is not the truth. The truth can only be found by viewing the videotape in the context of everything else that happened," said one of those Los Angeles cops, Stacey Koon.

The same was true of the Hall-Crosby confrontation. News reports said Crosby was an "honor student." That was not true. "Pharon decides when he wants to pay attention or work in class," said one teacher, who recalled how Crosby once threw a desk at him because he reprimanded him for sleeping in class.

When the case finally went to court, Crosby was convicted of resisting arrest. He also lost a civil suit and was ordered to pay an undisclosed amount for Hall's injuries. Nonetheless, the city surrendered and settled Crosby's lawsuit against the cops out of court by paying him $32,500 to avoid higher litigation expenses. It was "no admission whatsoever of police wrongdoing," according to the city solicitor who handled the case, Karl Kadon.

Stories at the time quoted protesters who labeled Hall as the white "racist" cop who attacked an innocent high school kid who was waiting for a bus. That was ironic. Hall is a Japanese-American who has felt the stinging barbs of bigotry and racism himself. Even a "tribute" cartoon from fellow cops showed him as the slant-eyed, toothy "Jap" stereotype. Hall was by all accounts a good cop with plenty of commendations, who was just doing his job, responding to complaints, trying to keep the streets safe for secretaries, CEOs and managers who were afraid to use the sidewalk in front of their own offices.

The reaction making Crosby "another Rodney King" was a preview of the city's response to riots six years later. In the Crosby confrontation, City Manager John Shirey folded like an overloaded paper plate and leaned on the police chief, Mike Snowden, to discipline or fire Hall. Snowden refused. Hall went back to duty while dueling lawsuits between the cop and Crosby snailed their way through the courts.

Six years later, on another hot April afternoon, bad luck put Sgt. Hall in command of Field Force Three, a team of SWAT officers dispatched to clear intersections and respond to arson, beatings and shootings on the day of the funeral of Timothy Thomas.

"Field Forces always got the worst assignments," said SWAT

Commander Lieutenant Doug Ventre.

They had seen what could happen when cars were trapped by a crowd in a blocked intersection. SWAT officer John Rose spoke for many cops when he described what he saw.

"There was one I recall that really bothered me a lot. We responded to 1305 Walnut, and there was this couple, elderly, about 65." Four years later, he still shakes his head in disbelief. "They were just beaten unbelievably and they were just laying there. I was infuriated. Their 'crime' was just going down the street being white. The news wouldn't report this stuff. If you excuse this kind of behavior, you will excuse anything. And they called it 'unrest' and 'rebellion.' Unrest!? I guess the word 'riot' just got lost."

SWAT Officers Tim Pappas and John Mercado were members of Hall's Field Force Three, which included six Cincinnati cops and two Ohio State Highway Patrol troopers. Pappas and Mercado had seen the same kinds of beatings during the riots. A crowd would block traffic, then the mob would pick one white victim's car at random, smash the car's windows with rocks and drag the driver and passengers into the street for a violent beating.

Field Force cops probably saved dozens of lives during the riots, following the same standard orders: teams of three to five squad cars, with two cops per car, were told to get there fast, form a perimeter, rescue the victims, disperse the crowds with beanbag shotguns, clear the intersection and "get the hell out" before the crowds of rioters washed back over the cops and trapped them.

The quick-response plan worked. By the Saturday of the funeral for Thomas, it was routine riot procedure, and Field Force teams were assigned as one of the layers of extra security to protect Ohio Gov. Bob Taft, who decided to attend the funeral despite warnings that it would put tremendous strain on the police.

As the funeral was coming to a close, a police helicopter surveillance team had reported that a gang of New Black Panthers was marching through the neighborhood. Police intelligence had picked up rumors that the Panthers were planning to shoot a cop. The police had already been shot at by snipers in the same neighborhood. SWAT officers working on Field Force Three were ordered by Lieutenant Jim Whalen to "clear the street" at Liberty and Elm, where blocked traffic was causing a hazard.

"There were fifty to seventy-five people in the intersection," Pappas said. "We used lights and hand gestures to warn them. We shouted to disperse and back up. They refused, and when we saw someone armed with a bottle we opened fire with beanbags, cleared the intersection and left."

Hall and Mercado told the same story. "I didn't see any women or any children," Hall said. "I scanned the areas. There was nobody on the ground that needed attention. The intersection was cleared, so we left. I didn't think anything of it."

"Bean-Bag Barrage Draws Scrutiny" the headlines said the next day. "Witnesses Saw No Reason for Shots."

Most news reports were based on accounts by a freelance Associated Press photographer, two women who were activists for Stonewall Cincinnati, and Christine Jones of Louisville.

But documents obtained from the FBI through a Freedom of Information Act request tell a different story.

Jones told the press, "People were just standing around talking, very peaceful." She said, "We weren't loud, we weren't yelling, we weren't doing anything."

But witnesses interviewed by the FBI, whose names were redacted, described Jones as one of the "fools" with a microphone, "hollering and cussing," "hyping the crowd," holding a banner in the middle of the street. Her group from Louisville was representing the "Kentucky Alliance Against Racist and Political Oppression and Citizens Against Police Abuse," a friend of Jones told the FBI.

One witness held the Jones group responsible for the incident. "When they clustered in the street and unfurled their banner, that had the effect of interfering with traffic. Because of the way they stretched across the intersection, many people who were walking down from the church got caught up in the situation."

Another witness from the Cincinnati Human Relations Commission said she saw several people in the neighborhood trying to incite violence. "They did not have peaceful intentions. They tried to mix with the large group to shield their presence from the police."

About thirty drug-gang members attended the funeral and were very vocal, she said. "These people were using a lot of profanity and cursing the clergy."

The FBI report described an interview with a witness: "She recalled that on three or four days she saw a white woman with dark, stringy hair trying to stir up crowds. This woman was not a peaceful protester. She was trying to incite people. (The witness) recalled thinking to herself that this woman was going to end up in trouble."

After the beanbags were fired and the police left, witnesses said Jones was seen angrily arguing with a TV camera crew. One saw "a white female who was bleeding from a wound to her hand caused by a beanbag. The woman was holding the beanbag . . . arguing with a news man . . . asking him why he had not gotten film of the confrontation."

News stories said Jones was hit with a beanbag and was treated in a Louisville hospital for a cracked rib, bruised spleen and bruised lung.

But Jones was first examined at the scene by Cincinnati paramedics, who took her to Good Samaritan Hospital in Cincinnati, where she was treated and released. X-rays at Good Samaritan showed no serious injuries.

Cecil Thomas, director of the Cincinnati Human Relations Commission, was in the street outside the funeral that day. "I was right in the middle of this—I will never forget it. There was a handful of five, maybe 10 people who were determined to incite the young folks and agitate this city for their own agenda.

"After the funeral, the kids were having their own makeshift memorial, and there was this older black lady who came up and she really got 'em revved up. She was shouting, 'We need to go downtown and tear it up,' and they took off in that direction.

"I walked over to her and said, 'I saw what you did. If you don't get down there and turn them around, I can guarantee you I will send you to the penitentiary for inciting a riot. She ran off and got 'em turned around. I'm sure she was not from Cincinnati."

He says he passed the area where the Beanbag incident occurred just before the cops pulled up. Jones was sitting on some porch steps when he walked past. "I got about 20 or 30 feet away and I heard a shot and I ran back and said 'Stop the shooting.' I didn't hear any warnings, and I wasn't that far away. I just think it was an overreaction by officers at that point."

To the cops who were working that day, it looked entirely different. City council members, the mayor and the governor of Ohio had gone into the red-hot center of the riot zone to attend an emotional funeral that stirred up anger and anti-police hatred. New Black Panthers, snipers, teens in bandit masks, protesters from Louisville—all of them were mixing with the peaceful mourners leaving the funeral, and a blocked intersection could be disaster if the governor's black Suburban was trapped and attacked.

Watching the governor of Ohio get yanked from his vehicle and beaten in the street was the cops' worst nightmare. To prevent that, they were ordered to clear the intersection.

Thomas says it took a God-given miracle to prevent more rioting that day. "We had organized a huge group of ministers from all over the region, gathered at Taft High School, right next to the First District Police headquarters.

"They were met by this angry crowd of young people coming in the other direction to go to the police headquarters. The kids got mixed into the ministers, because they thought they were all marching downtown to act up.

"I heard this minister say to one of them, 'Son, let me pray with you.' You could see these kids looking around like, 'Oh, no, we're not in the right place.' It took the steam right out of the situation. That was the thing that really turned everything around."

The cops still ask a good question: What were Jones and her Louisville caravan of protesters doing in Cincinnati that day? The cops and others who were there don't think she was injured by beanbags at all. They think she was cut by glass from a bottle hurled at the police.

But the city never tried to stand up for the cops and fight her lawsuit. Cincinnati City Council caved in to protesters, settled the case and paid $236,000 to the beanbag victims, which included two sisters, ages 7 and 11.

The "clear the intersection and clear out" tactic used so effectively during the riots became a "drive-by" attack on peaceful mourners. Soon the Beanbag Six cops were racking up $100,000 in legal fees to defend themselves from a Justice Department investigation requested by the mayor of Cincinnati.

In January 2002, Sgt. Eric Hall retired from the Cincinnati Police on a post-traumatic stress disability. He was having chest pains and constant anxiety about losing his house or being sent to prison. Eventually, he went to work as a campus police officer at the University of Cincinnati.

"I was just doing my job," he said near the end of 2002. "Don't ask me to deal with the violence of your riots and not support me."

But that's exactly what Cincinnati City Council did. Council members begged the cops to protect them from the rioters, and then as soon as the violence began to subside the politicians turned their backs on the cops and joined the "police brutality" protesters who wanted to lynch the Bean-bag Six.

The police slowdown began when politicians offered up Hall, Mercado, Pappas and the rest of Field Force Three as a sacrifice to protesters. For Eric Hall, it was a career-killer. The good cop who had wanted to be a policeman all his life had to quit the job he loved. For Hall, the police slowdown was complete—his career as a cop came to a stop. A lot of other cops saw what happened to him and the other SWAT officers—the best, toughest, most highly trained cops in CPD—and decided that doing "the job" aggressively was not worth the risk. Some quit the SWAT team in protest.

During the following years, crime and drug-gang killings exploded and the exodus began, as longtime Cincinnati cops took early retirement or better jobs somewhere else, and middle-class residents who could afford to move out packed up and fled the city.

"Just let us do it," Mercado said looking back, voicing the frustration shared by many cops. "Just support the police and let us do everything we can to clean up the streets and we will do it. Just let us do it."

During the worst rioting, firemen and
paramedics needed police escorts to protect
them as they rescued victims of beatings
and people injured by rock-throwing mobs.

CHAPTER 12

THE MOUTH
THAT ROARED

As a crowd gathered on the street in front of City Hall, a man climbed up on top of a car with a bullhorn and started shouting to encourage a protest over police shootings. A few days later, nearly 1,000 people packed a City Council meeting for an angry and emotional racial confrontation.

But the year was not 2001. It was 1979. The protesters were not civil rights leaders and black citizens, they were Cincinnati cops, led by a tall man with Elvis sideburns and a white cowboy hat—the flamboyant, incendiary president of the Fraternal Order of Police, Elmer Dunaway.

Dunaway, a part-time cosmetologist and full-time Cincinnati policeman who became FOP president in 1972, was called arrogant, insolent and a bully. He organized and led the first police slowdowns in Cincinnati during contract negotiations, extracting—some said extorting—raises that pushed police salaries from $10,000 to $25,000 by the time he lost the office 15 years later.

He was the first to use endorsements to take the FOP into politics. He called liberal judges communists and accused political opponents on city council of coddling criminals. When a black suspect was accused of shooting a white cop, Dunaway told the press, "I'd like to make the arrest. He'd never go to trial."

For statements like that, he got a nickname: The Mouth that Roared.

But Dunaway had a cause that still reverberates with cops in Cincinnati 20 years later. When he climbed on top of a police cruiser outside City Hall in May of 1979, three cops had been killed in two months. Eight had been killed since 1974. After the funeral that day for Officer Mel Henze, who was shot in his cruiser, the cowboy FOP president led a motorcade of cops to City Hall, where they jammed on their brakes and locked their cruisers, some with lights still flashing. They then marched a few blocks to the Police Memorial across from the First District Police Headquarters and threw their car keys at the base of the monument to fallen officers. Twenty-two years later, rioters pulled down the flags at the same police memorial.

That one-day police strike led to a confrontation at City Hall a few days later, when cops and their families packed the council meeting, which also overflowed with black community leaders and civil rights activists.

Dunaway was there to demand bigger guns to replace obsolete police-issue .38s. He demanded bullet-proof vests, and asked council members to "get the damned shotguns out of the trunks." Police policy at the time required cops to keep their shotguns locked in the trunks of their cruisers.

Cincinnati's black community remembers it well, like a scar from a bullet wound. During a shouting contest at the meeting, a cop yanked the necktie of the Cincinnati NAACP President, nearly setting off a brawl at City Hall.

The Police Chief resigned from the FOP the next day, and some high-ranking cops said Dunaway should be charged with inciting a riot. Civil rights leaders called him a racist. Editorials condemned him for instigating a strike that jeopardized public safety. Hamilton County Common Please Judge Gilbert Bettman deplored Dunaway for "vicious, intemperate, public and personal attacks" on Cincinnati's first black mayor, Ted Berry, who had criticized the city's "arrogant" cops.

Dunaway replied that maintaining morale among Cincinnati cops was difficult while "five or six council members kick their heads year in and year out."

He could have been talking about the aftermath of the 2001 riots.

Dunaway got what he wanted. Today, Cincinnati cops carry more powerful 9 mm semi-automatics that give them a better chance against the .357 magnums and automatic weapons used by drug thugs. They have bullet-proof vests and shotguns are now locked in the front seat of cruisers, easy to grab in a shootout.

But Elmer Dunaway achieved something else that even he probably never expected. He didn't just raise salaries, he raised the stakes. He turned the FOP into a more powerful weapon in the battle between civil rights leaders and law enforcement. And he put the leader of the FOP in a new position, in the front seat, always handy for a political gunfight.

After Dunaway was replaced in 1987, rank-and-file cops chose a series of leaders who took lower profiles, who negotiated and cooperated with police brass and city council.

But when attacks on police escalated in the press and political arena during the mid-1990s, they turned to a new leader who was in the Dunaway mold. In 1997, while civil rights leaders, the press and council members were accusing the Cincinnati Police of using excessive force in arrests and confrontations with black males, the FOP elected Keith Fangman as president.

Fangman quickly went on the attack and spoke publicly about "anti-police bias" in the media, on city council and among black community activists.

In 1996, when civil rights lawyer Ken Lawson erroneously accused cops of beating a suspect to death, Fangman said, "What ticks me off is that those reckless, inflammatory statements, those lies . . . could have easily caused a riot in this city."

It was prophetic.

"One of the things I ran on was the need to be more vocal," he said. He kept his promise. Fangman was to vocal what Dunaway was to cowboy hats. It was the first thing you noticed.

During the riots and their aftermath, Fangman was the leader who would not back down. He went on national news networks to debate national civil rights leaders the Rev. Al Sharpton and national NAACP President Kweise Mfumi. And while those critics of Cincinnati and its cops often spread exaggerations and misinformation, Fangman more than held his own in the talk-show rodeo.

His arguments could have been lifted directly from Dunaway more than 20 years earlier: Yes, black men are getting shot for resisting arrest and assaulting cops—but what about all the cops who have been killed by black men in Cincinnati? What about the crime?

During the riots, Fangman was deplored like Dunaway for pointing out that 90 percent of the violent crime, 95 percent of assaults on cops, 93 percent of murders and 90 percent of rapes were committed by less than 40 percent of the city population—black males. That upset Cincinnati's business and political leaders.

"I was told, 'Shhhh, Keith. Be quiet.' I was under a lot of pressure. I said you can go to hell. I was not elected to sugarcoat the truth or play footsies with police critics."

And when the Department of Justice opened a secret grand jury investigation of "The Beanbag Six," to pressure the cops to testify against each other or go to prison for civil rights violations, Fangman picked up a phone and booked a flight to Washington, D.C.

Six months later, when the DOJ team from D.C. suddenly closed down their grand jury, packed up and left town without warning, a spokesman said they decided to drop the investigation because it would be too hard to bring indictments against police officers in the post-9-11 climate of national respect and appreciation for the police heroes who gave their lives in the World Trade Center attack.

To anyone who listened closely, that sounded like a lame excuse. Media reports hinted that there must be another reason—but none of the reporters came up with plausible explanation or a source who would tell what really happened.

Five years later, Fangman told the story of the behind-the-scenes political poker that forced the DOJ to fold and shut down their investigation.

"The national media was reporting that mourners leaving the church were shot with beanbags," Fangman recalled. "It was an absolute lie."

So was the story about the 9-11 climate, he said.

"They wanted to prove that Ashcroft was not a racist so they overcompensated. They were going to hang these cops."

U.S. Attorney General John Ashcroft had barely survived scorching confirmation hearings, during which Democrats accused him of being racist because he had voted against Ronnie White, a black judge nominated for a lifetime federal judicial appointment by President Bill Clinton.

Ashcroft had very good reasons to oppose the nomination of Judge White. He knew the judge from his home state of Missouri. White had tried to block the execution of cop-killer James Johnson, who ambushed and killed a sheriff and three deputies, then shot the sheriff's wife while she was conducting a Bible study in her home.

Ashcroft called Judge White a "pro-criminal" judicial activist who set records for trying to block death penalties. White was one of the few Clinton appointees rejected by the Senate. Both Missouri senators voted against him.

But in the world of Washington's partisan trench combat, that gave

Democrats all they needed to call Ashcroft a racist when his own nomination for attorney general by President Bush went to Senate hearings.

Fangman began to suspect Ashcroft's motives after his first visit to Washington. "I had two meetings with Ralph Boyd," the head of the DOJ's civil rights division. "It was obvious he was under orders from higher up to hang the cops."

A lame-duck Cincinnati U.S. Attorney appointed by President Clinton, Sharon Zealey, had pushed for the beanbag investigation by going over the heads of the local FBI, Fangman and local FBI agents said. "The FBI told me the DOJ wanted indictments to make Ashcroft look good."

Fangman leveraged the first meeting with Boyd by contacting the national FOP, which had come out with a surprise endorsement of Republican President Bush, helping to deliver his narrow victory over Al Gore. "During his campaign, Bush had assured the FOP that 'If I'm elected, my Justice Department will not act as the internal affairs division for local policing,'" Fangman said.

The meeting with Boyd did not go well. "He obviously did not want to hear what I had to say."

So Fangman escalated. He was contacted in mid-summer by reporters from the *New York Times* and *Washington Post*, to be quoted in stories about the aftermath of the riots. "That's when the light bulb went on," he said. "They were trying to get me to accuse Bush and Ashcroft. The national media was chomping at the bit to find out what's really going on here. We had six innocent cops getting railroaded to make Bush and Ashcroft look like heroes."

So Fangman went back to the national FOP leadership to lean on Boyd for another meeting. His message: "Tell them that unless they meet with me, I'm going to call a press conference."

He says he told Boyd, "Unless you call it off, I'm going to blow the lid off it and tell every reporter who will listen, and every cop in the country will look at Cincinnati and see what's happening. Within 72 hours, the grand jury was disbanded. I promised I would not gloat or do interviews."

Police Chief Tom Streicher had a similar complaint for the FBI. During a dinner in 2005, he told the local FBI Agent in Charge, "You guys are our friends until the big-foot politicians come to town, then you're ready to crucify an innocent cop to give them what they want."

Mayor Charlie Luken also said the Fangman explanation makes sense.

When Ashcroft visited Cincinnati to sign a memorandum of understanding between the city and the DOJ, "He obviously wanted to spend more time talking to (boycott leader) Damon Lynch than anyone else," he said. "I thought to myself at the time that Ashcroft is getting something out of this."

Ashcroft refused to answer any questions.

DOJ lawyers were tight-lipped about their reasons for leaving town suddenly. But a couple of years later, when Cincinnati Congressman Steve Chabot told the DOJ to back off and stop handcuffing Cincinnati Police with nitpicking rules, Boyd angrily denied that the political pressure had any effect and complained bitterly about suggestions that political pressure had forced the DOJ to back down.

Perhaps the best indication of the DOJ's decision came from one of their spokesmen when they announced they were closing down the investigation and disbanding the grand jury. "My hope is that the FOP will take this as a positive decision."

But the DOJ lawyers deliberately left the cops in limbo, refusing to publicly declare them innocent, although other investigations found that they did everything they were supposed to do, by the book, and may have prevented another outbreak of violence and rioting on the day of an emotional funeral.

Nearly a year after they were accused and dragged into court, the beanbag cops were finally cleared, and City Council reluctantly paid their legal bills, as required by city policy.

Fangman and the FOP had delivered. The police union that was not even political before 1972 had become a national player to be reckoned with, even winning a stud-poker showdown with the U.S. Attorney General.

Fangman did something else, too. Quietly, without publicity or fanfare, he persuaded Police Chief Tom Streicher to bring back the old, traditional arm patch on Cincinnati Police uniforms. It had been replaced by former Police Chief Mike Snowden with a more family-friendly blue and gold patch depicting the skyline, the Roebling Suspension Bridge and a steamboat in the Ohio River—known among cops as "the King's Island patch," after the local amusement park.

The old patch, which is now back in service, is no tourism brochure. It's gold on black, showing an eagle in front of an American flag, its talons clutching a sword and a shield.

   Elmer Dunaway would be proud.

Police Chief Thomas Streicher took a seat
at the Law and Public Safety Committee
meeting on April 9 and tried to answer
questions as he was shouted at by an angry
crowd. Standing directly behind him is
Lt. Col. Vincent DeMasi.

CHAPTER 13

THE LAST
WORD

P olice Chief Thomas Streicher was driving through the winter-bleached corn stubble of Indiana. It was Sunday morning, April 8, 2001. He was coming home to Cincinnati from a three-day Police Research Forum in Chicago. And as he drove along the nearly empty highway, he picked up his cell phone and called police headquarters to leave a message for First District Commander Vince DiMasi.

"Vince picked up and I asked, 'What the hell are you doing in the office on Sunday morning?' There was this pause and he said, 'You don't know what happened.' I said 'No.' He said, 'We killed a guy.'

"I said 'We, as in police?' He said yes, and described what happened."

It was more than 24 hours after the shooting of Timothy Thomas by Police Officer Stephen Roach, and the chief of police was being informed for the first time, merely by accident.

DiMasi gave Streicher a rough outline of the events and Roach's story, and Streicher got a funny feeling right away. "I killed a guy in 1980, so I know something about police shootings. The first thing I said is 'It's bull.' He said, 'I think so too.'"

÷÷÷

At the corner of Boudinot and Westwood Northern Boulevard on the West Side of Cincinnati, the car wash is still there. It's now named "Tom's Car Wash."

"How ironic is that?" Streicher says, easing his black Ford 500 into the parking lot, past the edge of a building and through a narrow alley above and beside the bays where wands hang in holsters on the wall near the coin-operated suds, wax and rinse controls.

"The post is still there. It was right here," he says on a fall afternoon in 2005, pointing to a dark steel post set in the blacktop. "I told the investigators there was no light, but everyone else said, 'No, Tom, the lights were on.' Later I came back to check it out, and they were right. It was lit up so bright you could see across the road and 20 feet into the woods over there. They told me I had tunnel vision—a classic case."

Soldiers, doctors, coaches and cops say tunnel vision is related to perceptual narrowing, a cortical process, and occurs in some individuals during acute stress. In battle, military commanders know gunners must be protected with covering fire because they sometimes can only see what is directly in front of them, making them vulnerable to attacks from the flanks. Peripheral vision is blacked out. Only a narrow tunnel is visible, making a sort of spotlight in a dark auditorium, where the focus is often in great detail, sometimes in slow motion.

That's how Streicher remembers the night he shot a drug dealer in 1980. Great detail. Slow motion. Tattooed on his memory like a scene from his own private movie.

"I was at a wedding reception this summer and it popped into my head. I lived right through the whole thing again and then it popped back out. I wondered, 'Twenty-five years later? What the hell?'"

In 1980, he was working with an undercover narcotics team—long-hair wigs, beards, scruffy clothes. "We heard from an informant that there were some guys out there with a lot of dope, and we figured we could catch them as they came into the city."

They made contact, and made a deal to buy $400 worth of Quaaludes, an illegal muscle relaxant that was popular as a "recreational drug" at the time. The 'ludes salesman got in the unmarked car with three cops posing as buyers. Streicher was at the wheel, heading for the car wash parking lot where they had made buys before. A second car carrying the drug-dealer's friends followed.

"He said he was just out of prison. He told us he had a gun, 'and if anything goes wrong, no matter whose fault, I'm gonna end it, I'm gonna kill everybody, and you're first, driver.'"

They stopped in the lot and one of the cops, Floyd Lanter, pretended to head for the bushes to "take a leak." As the undercover team moved into position to set up crossfire around the dealer, Lanter took a spot toward the back of the car driven by Streicher, to cover the people in the car behind them. "At a prearranged signal, we would yell 'Police' and make the arrest. I had worked my pistol out of my pants and had my gun on him."

Streicher was standing near the right front headlight—the drug suspect was across the hood of the car, next to a steel post set in asphalt.

Someone yelled "Police." And the suspect plunged his hand into his jacket where he had earlier pointed to his gun.

"He froze and looked at me, straight face, a very blank look on his face. Then he looked back at Floyd, and then back at me. Suddenly he got this wild-eyed look on his face and turned toward Floyd, and I thought, 'Oh, no, he's gonna get Floyd."

Streicher started shooting, then, "I hit the ground and heard a scream. But when I got up again, he was still standing there. I can't believe I missed. Then he pulled his hand out all covered with blood. He looked at me and—boom—he hit the ground. I ran over and he took three breaths and he was dead. The bullet had severed his aorta."

Streicher can still see the cops running in slow motion, looking for the gun. "They told me 'There's no gun.' He had just been faking it with his hand."

To make it worse, the dead suspect, Gary Bevins, turned out to be the nephew of one of the cops on the scene.

"You cannot believe how vivid it still is. I still get emotional when I talk about it. I sit down with young cops who have been through this and I tell them here's what I personally experienced. Don't think you are crazy when you experience it over and over and over and over in your head. It won't stop."

"You're threat perception is so strong, it's like a thermometer in a cartoon that goes so high it blows up. The fear and threat is so strong, the training kicks in."

Twenty-five years later, Streicher has been involved as an investigator or commander in 95 percent of the shooting incidents involving CPD. And he has developed an instinct for making the right call.

Something wasn't right in the story DiMasi told about Roach and Thomas. "It was too textbook perfect. I usually know if a shooting is right or wrong in three to five minutes. You look at the evidence, listen to the story. You get a gut feeling."

His gut feeling this time was that Roach's story was false. He told DiMasi to scour the city and collect all of the new video cameras that had been recently installed in police cruisers that responded to the scene of the shooting, on the remote chance something had been caught on tape. Early Monday morning, April 9, he assembled his top commanders in his office, and started the meeting with a question: "What did we tell them at the first press conference?"

He was met with an awkward silence and blank stares. Finally, someone said, "We didn't have one."

Streicher was amazed. "You mean we had a Friday night shooting and killed a guy and now it's Monday and nobody has spoken?"

They shook their heads and studied the carpet.

For two critical days, as the city's trouble thermometer climbed and threatened to explode, nobody told the chief and nobody talked to the press. If someone had called him in Chicago, "I'd a got up and left. I would've been home in six hours," he said.

But Streicher was amazed that nothing was done by the assistant chief he had left in charge, Lieutenant Colonel Ron Twitty.

Streicher called a press conference to get out all the information the police had. Then as he got ready to leave for City Hall, DiMasi called with surprising news: "We got the whole shooting on tape."

The chief asked: Did it match Roach's version?

"It ain't even close," DiMasi replied.

Streicher thought, "Oh, no, now I have to go to Law and Public Safety." There would be no time to review the tape before he was thrust into the spotlight to explain what really happened.

He expected the council meeting to be tense and emotional. He had no idea it had already erupted in chaos. Nobody had informed the police about the meeting agenda or told Streicher what to expect. Uniformed officers who might have warned headquarters were ordered by council members to stay out.

On his way to the meeting, Streicher was in a jam. "If I tell people what I know, we compromise the criminal investigation and we will never get to the bottom of anything," he thought.

And then he walked into a maelstrom that looked like the end of city government—but it was only the beginning of the riots.

÷÷÷

Streicher is the last Cincinnati Police Chief protected by state civil service rules from arbitrary firing and political pressure. A hasty post-riot reform called Issue 5 took away the protection from political meddling and opened the job to outsiders—an effort to "change the culture" of the police division. But wherever the next chief comes from, he will have a hard time replacing the loved and respected chief affectionately known to beat cops as "Tommy."

Through storms, insults and name-calling attacks, Streicher has always kept his cool. He responds with the poker-faced, neutral, polite demeanor of a professional cop doing an unpleasant traffic stop with an obnoxious speeder.

"After all these years of being a cop, do they think there's a name I haven't been called?" he laughs. "There is never a time to publicly 'lose it.' Never let them see you mad. If you mess up, 'fess up—and fix it. If I lose it and sink to that level, then the issue becomes me and they say 'See, that's why cops are the way they are.'"

Streicher is slim, medium height, so clean-cut it's hard to even imagine him in undercover long hair and beard. He's the son of a Cincinnati Police detective, a West Sider who went to Elder High School—which has a reputation for turning out cops the way Cincinnati's Moeller High School has a reputation for turning out Big Ten football players.

An old saying in Cincinnati goes, "East Siders make the money—and West Siders watch it." It's mostly true. Judges, prosecutors and cops are nearly always West Siders. Bankers and CEOs come from the East Side.

After the riots, a new member of council, Christopher Smitherman, wanted to investigate how many cops may have attended Elder High School like Streicher, as if being from the West Side was some kind of crime. As of 2005, the councilman was gone, but Streicher, who jokes about being a stubborn German, was still on the job.

÷ ÷ ÷

Since 2001, the chief has traveled the nation presenting the lessons from the Cincinnati riots to other police departments and cities. He has shared his own department's mistakes and successes with a roundtable of the top 50 urban police chiefs who represent 65 percent of all the cops in America.

"One of our biggest mistakes was zero communication. That let the city start boiling," he tells them.

There was no communication outside the department to share facts and details, and no communication inside the department to even inform the chief about the shooting.

Another lesson from Cincinnati is that curfews work. At first, Streicher told Mayor Charlie Luken a curfew was not really necessary. "Who the hell is going to listen to a curfew when they're robbing, looting and shooting at each other?

"The air was filled with smoke, fire engines going both ways down the street followed by our cars giving support. Shots are going off, bottles and rocks are flying. I can't tell you how many times I was pelted with rocks and bottles. I was thinking, 'Am I going to wake up? Is this real?'"

"We had arson, robbery and rape. So who cares about a misdemeanor curfew?"

But it worked. When it finally went into effect on Thursday at 8 p.m., "It was like someone turned off the switch. We were dumfounded."

Reinforcements from the Ohio State Troopers and the Hamilton County Sheriff's Department helped too.

Streicher warns other police chiefs about the ragged deterioration of decision making after hours without sleep, working 20-hour days. "At times I knew I had to take action, but I couldn't even think, and then you let it go and move to the next thing."

Non-lethal beanbag shotguns and cops on horses saved lives and saved the city, he says.

But the lesson that has gone unspoken in Cincinnati since those days in April 2001 may be the most obvious to everyone except the press and political leaders who never "got it."

Say "thank you" to the cops who lay their lives on the line to save your city. Support them. Let them do their job.

"Never, ever was there said a single word of gratitude to us for anything," Streicher said. "Quite honestly, we never expected it. We knew we would be chastised and publicly humiliated by city council."

But he didn't expect the attack on the police to start during the riots, before the fires were put out.

÷÷÷

On Friday night, as the week of lawless violence was finally being pushed back in its bottle, Streicher was just leaving the scene of another skirmish when he got a call at 6:07 p.m. City officials wanted him to meet with a

U.S. Department Justice team they had invited to the city to scrutinize the police.

They told him to be there at 6:15. No problem, he thought. He was coming to work hours earlier than that the next morning, anyway.

No, they said. They meant 6:15 p.m.—that evening. Seven minutes.

He replied, "Do they know we have a riot going on?"

He was given the oldest lie in the encyclopedia of mendacity: The federal government is here to help.

"I'd been up a whole lot by that time, and I was not in a mood to listen to B.S.," he remembers. But that's what he got. Seven minutes to prepare for a meeting to discuss training, recruitment, minority hiring, use of force, promotion policies, weapons deployment and other bureaucratic policy issues.

Streicher soon found out the DOJ team had talked to everyone else first—civil rights activists, protesters, ACLU lawyers, city council, critics of the cops, even the Sentinels association of black patrol officers.

"They came to town with a preconceived notion that our entire operation was wrong. That's why the meeting was a failure and that's why (federal oversight) is a failure to this day."

Later, Streicher found out the team included DOJ's top headhunter who was sent to add the scalps of a few Cincinnati cops to his trophy collection. The meeting that Friday evening slid downhill quickly and deteriorated from there.

Eventually, the DOJ went after the Beanbag Six officers. And when the DOJ team hit a dead-end and couldn't bring indictments for civil rights violations, they sent a local FBI agent to pressure Streicher, he says.

That led to a confrontational meeting he has never talked about before.

The agent wanted Streicher to lean on the cops to plead to misdemeanors, he said, shaking his head, still angry. "That's when I realized I was also the subject of their investigation, that they were after me all along. What a pelt that would have been to have the police chief trying to cover up the beanbag incident."

Streicher told the agent, "You've been trying to indict me, haven't you? And now that you can't, you want me to pressure my cops to plead to misdemeanors. You want to find a political answer—to sacrifice my cops. But I'll tell you right now that I will testify that those officers did exactly what

I trained them to do. Take that to a jury. Now get the f— out of my office."

The agent told Streicher, "Don't get mad at the messenger. We've been friends up till now."

That only confirmed it for him; the political pressure was coming from higher up. And it taught him a lesson he has not forgotten. "Local cops are expendable to the feds."

The feds and the Cincinnati police were not good friends after that. They worked together only when they had to. Streicher's angry opinion of the FBI was, "They couldn't find a bleeding elephant in the snow."

"But if I had to handpick people to protect the president of the United States, I would choose those beanbag cops. That's how good they are."

The FBI backed off. The DOJ team packed up its expandable files and heavy briefcases of paperwork and left town without warning. But the assault on the Cincinnati Police was just beginning.

The cops who held the line against rioters were now under attack from a new direction: commissions, politicians, monitors, ACLU lawyers, protesters, reporters, politicians and federal judges.

"They never acknowledged that the police division functioned exactly the way it was designed to do. We made the right call. That never came out."

The cop who shot Thomas, Stephen Roach, was prosecuted and forced to leave Cincinnati Police, although he was acquitted in court and eventually became a highly regarded Evendale Police officer. "I frankly was flabbergasted that he was found not guilty," Streicher said.

He's still amazed at the attitude of Cincinnati's leaders, too.

"How can people take one isolated incident, one officer involved in a shooting, and extrapolate that to say that's the way Cincinnati Police Department operates?

"It's ridiculous. You'd think the media would be stepping forward to say that rioting is intolerable, that whatever injustice has happened in the past, that's never justification for looting and assaults."

Tom Streicher agonizes about what happened, just as he still relives the shooting in a car wash parking lot 25 years ago. He has a simple question for the leaders of Cincinnati:

"How in God's name can anybody ever say the riots were the fault of the police?"

Property damage from the riots
was estimated at $12 million.

CHAPTER 14

LESSONS FROM RIOT SCHOOL

At the top of a landing leading to the fourth floor, light spills down onto the worn white marble stairs through the most spectacular stained glass window at City Hall. It shows Cincinnatus, the soldier-farmer who saved Rome, being approached by a delegation of politicians who are trying to hand him the "fasces," an ax that was the symbol of dictatorship. According to legend, Cincinnatus returned, led Rome in battle, defeated the Aequi and the Volscians and returned to his farm before his fresh-plowed furrows could sprout—all in 16 days.

But the Cincinnatus in stained glass does not look enthusiastic about going back to run Rome. He stands with one hand on his plow, reluctant to interrupt his work. His other arm is folded across his brow. He could be wiping away the sweat of honest toil—or he could be putting his forearm to his forehead in the classic gesture of resigned dismay: "Oh, Zeus, not again."

From where he stands in that window, he can look directly down onto the City Council chambers, and see everything that happened after the riots of 2001. He probably saw it coming—shielding his eyes with resigned disgust.

÷÷÷

Federal Judge Susan Dlott could often be seen pushing a covered baby carriage down the polished halls of the John Peck Federal Building at Walnut and Vine streets downtown. But anyone who peeked in was in for a shock. Her "babies" had long noses, sharp teeth and long, shedding hair. They were fluffy lap dogs, Dickens and Crumpet, two Cavalier King Charles Spaniels, to be specific.

In her office, the furniture was overrun with dog statues, ceramic dogs, wood-carved dogs, pictures of dogs and stuffed animal dogs. They even crowded out pictures of Bill and Hillary Clinton. Dlott, a former U.S. Attorney with no judicial experience, was appointed to the federal bench by Clinton in 1995 after many friendly visits to the Clinton White House with her big-donor husband, super lawyer Stan Chesley.

"Eccentric," a few brave lawyers might say when asked about Judge Dlott. Off the record, some would dare to say her dogs were a disgrace to the court. They ran free in her courtroom. And if one of them had an "accident" in court, one of Dlott's law clerks would be there in a trice with a handy paper towel and spray bottle to clean it up, without even a recess or objection.

U.S. marshals who run all visitors through metal detectors at the courthouse doors stand only a few feet away from a sign that says all animals are prohibited in the building unless they are material to a case in progress. It's a federal law. Apparently, it did not apply to federal judge Susan Dlott.

Ask the marshals about the time Dlott made them deputize her dogs and pose for a picture with them, and they get a stony look on their faces. She thought it was cute. They thought it was insulting and demeaning.

When she upheld Christmas as a federal holiday, her opinion was written in Dr. Seuss doggerel. And among Cincinnati law enforcement officials, she was notorious for being the most anti-cop judge on the federal bench, who once wondered in open court if testimony by police officers could be trusted. That was not cute, either. It was as demeaning as making her law clerks walk her dogs on taxpayer time, carrying pooper-scoopers.

Some said Dlott was an excellent judge. Some said she was a disgrace to the bench. But whatever they said, she was the new boss of the Cincinnati Police Division.

When Cincinnati City Council was stampeded by rioting into settling a flimsy class action lawsuit over alleged racial profiling by police, the case was handled by Dlott. And when council members agreed to sign on to what the press named "the historic collaborative agreement" to end racial profiling, it was Dlott who took the case and ushered in a small army of consultants, experts, conflict resolution specialists, monitors and expense-account racial faith healers.

And when it was time to choose a "monitor" to police the police under

Dlott's supervision, she chose her old friend "Dr. Kal." Alan Kalmanoff, who was not a physician but a PhD who insisted on the "Dr." tag, was a Berkeley, California, consultant who fit Cincinnati like hip-hugger bell-bottoms on John Wayne. It was a match made in hell.

Dr. Kal began feeding his meter as soon as he got Dlott's call. He billed Cincinnati for phone calls, for packing his suitcases with stuffed shirts and for every lengthy conversation with reporters. He even tried to bill the city for having dinner with Dlott. Some friend.

It only took a few phone calls to find out he had left a wake of dissatisfaction, acrimony, complaints about shoddy work and exorbitant bills in cities that had hired him before Cincinnati.

City council fired him. And Dlott appointed a new monitor, Saul Green, who came from a city that was a model of race relations—Detroit. Then Green and his team of "experts" quickly began running up Kalmanesque bills for dinners, taxis, waiting in airports, phone calls from reporters, ride-alongs with cops and long phone calls to each other.

The city funded the Historic Collaborative to the tune of $1 million a year and got in return—precisely nothing.

Dlott allowed one party—the Black United Front—to walk away from their obligations to the agreement. Then again, she had never asked them to explain exactly who the Black United Front was, or name their members or tell her how many people they represented. But the police, the city and the Fraternal Order of Police remained welded to the "process," forced to submit to a parade of imported "experts."

The Collaborative was hailed in the local media as a miracle cure for the race relations migraine. It was supposed to be a mutual agreement to improve police-community relations by holding both sides accountable. But it quickly became obvious that the black "community" and the plaintiffs—the ACLU and the Black United Front leader the Rev. Damon Lynch III—were invulnerable to accountability.

"The only organization whose feet were held to the fire is the police department," said Police Chief Thomas Streicher. "The plaintiffs were never held accountable and never criticized by the monitor."

The monitor's recommendations brought minor reforms to police dog policies. "That had nothing to do with anything that happened during the riots," Streicher said. Just a year before the monitor's criticism, the Cincinnati Police K-9 Unit had won the National Championship from the

U.S. Police Canine Association.

Green consistently refused to return phone calls. That may have been a blessing, because his conversations with reporters were billed to the city along with every other waking detail during his "work" on the collaborative.

Mayor Charlie Luken finally got fed up and suggested that the monitor and his team should pack up and leave. He implied that the whole charade was a lawyer-employment scheme by the ACLU. "The civil rights lawyers have got to find something to justify their existence," he said. "These lawyers in part make a living by suing the city. They will never acknowledge that the police are in compliance."

Streicher went a step further. In late December, 2004, he was scheduled to meet with one of Green's monitors, Rana Sampson of California. Cincinnati Police Lieutenant Colonel Richard Janke said Sampson's police experience on the street would not qualify her to hold a clipboard for one of his street lieutenants. But she was there to tell the chief how to run his department.

Police said Sampson requested a meeting without offering a reason or an agenda. She opened a notebook, said "OK" and sat there, Janke said. When Streicher asked what the purpose of the meeting was, she did not respond. When he asked other questions, she finally told him, "I don't work for you."

That did it. Streicher asked her to leave the building and canceled her scheduled ride-along with one of his top commanders. Sampson complained to Green, who held the city in "noncompliance," and Green complained to Dlott, who threatened to hold the police in contempt. In a memo, the police replied that Sampson repeatedly said she would not give CPD a clean report card until "drug markets" were eradicated "by means other than arrest," which she scorned as "traditional" law enforcement.

"They told us we should be able to police and stop crime without making any arrests," Streicher said. "Great."

÷ ÷ ÷

The Historic Collaborative shakedown may have been the worst riot solution, but it was not the first. Long before the monitors brought their road show to Cincinnati, another consultant was already in town to help with the "healing."

Immediately after the riots, the city's first black city manager, Sylvester Murray, was hired as a consultant by the non-profit KnowledgeWorks Foundation, at the request of Mayor Charlie Luken and with an endorsement by former mayor and Ohio Secretary of State Ken Blackwell, to "address the systemic issues relating to race relations"—consultant lingo for "root causes."

He was paid $1,440 a day and ran up a hotel bill of $4,716. He collected $130,000 for 12 days of visits. And when it was over, a lawsuit by KnowledgeWorks said he had "failed to do all of the work," billed "for work not done and expenses not incurred" and "failed to provide . . . periodic written reports" required by his contract. The court rejected Murray's claim for yet more money.

Then there was Luken's CAN commission, Cincinnati Action Now. It became an oil and water mix of the old Cincinnati way of closing all meetings to the press and public, and the new Cincinnati way of paralysis by inclusion. The unwieldy meetings were led by giant committees composed of virtually anyone who had a grievance against the city, or any social service agency that could cure race problems if only it got enough grants, spending and programs to address the root causes of riots.

The CAN commission was crippled from the start by Luken's choice of leaders. Tom Cody, an executive from Procter & Gamble was a popular and logical choice. But then Luken also picked the Rev. Damon Lynch III, who helped instigate rioting and led a race boycott against the city. Lynch grudgingly agreed to help. But he was soon kicked off the CAN by Luken when Lynch refused to give up his boycott and sent out a letter falsely accusing local police of raping and murdering blacks.

Luken also chose Ross Love, owner of WDBZ, the radio station that even Luken blamed for aggravating riot violence with incendiary talk show hosts such as Love's son, Jay Love.

Councilman Jim Tarbell said he asked Ross Love at an early CAN meeting how he could reconcile his role as healer when his station was still pouring turpentine into the open wounds and spreading untrue accusations about the city and its police. "He didn't answer me and I was never invited back," Tarbell said.

Chief Streicher attended "virtually every single" CAN meeting, as large groups would gather to talk "pie in the sky" solutions. "Everybody had the answer and it was always the same—it was the police department's fault," he said.

"They didn't want to hear about the rules and regulations we have to operate by. They wanted to make their own. They'd talk about diversity and how we needed diversity, and I'd explain that we are under something called a court-ordered consent decree, with three different hiring lists, one for minorities, one for females and one for whites. I explained that we are the most diverse police division in our region of the country, and that I don't have any control over hiring. I couldn't promote who I wanted to promote. They didn't want to hear it."

CAN began with a shopping list of programs that would bankrupt the state of California—and whittled that down to a shorter list that was merely unrealistic. Eventually, Love declared victory and turned out the lights, and CAN took its place in the Blue Ribbon Commission Museum: Cincinnati Action Never.

CAN could honestly claim one dubious success: in 2003, voters passed Issue 5, a Charter change to allow the police chief and top assistants to be hired by a national search, outside the civil service rules that required selection from within the department. Issue 5 ran head-on into the FOP police contract, however, and became a tangled mess of lawsuits. Years later, police promotions were still blocked by litigation and the police chief wondered, "How many of the businesses in this town could get by with 50 percent of their command staff vacant?"

As seen from behind the badge, Issue 5 was one more assault on the integrity and morale of the police who saved the city.

÷÷÷

After years of so-called solutions, lawsuits, court hearings and reports, at a cost of about $10 million that could have been spent hiring more police to reduce rising crime, Cincinnati remains about where it was before the riots.

"We're just a rock or a thrown bottle away from the whole thing going off again," said Cincinnati Human Relations Director Cecil Thomas in 2005. SWAT team members agreed. WDBZ talk show host Lincoln Ware agreed. Police Chief Tom Streicher agreed. So did council members and citizens who were not blinded by the rose-colored glasses they put on to sign the Historic Collaborative Agreement.

The reasons should be mandatory reading for any city that could have race riots—which is any city.

Cincinnati handed over its megaphone the same way Lieutenant Colonel Ron Twitty handed over his bullhorn to rioters. The city gave up its public-address apparatus to the voices of violence and division.

City council gave up its platform to protesters at the Law and Public Safety meeting that was broadcast citywide.

The media gave up its front pages to the boycotters and rioters, allowing them to say anything, no matter how incendiary or untrue, and gave them headlines for months, supplying the media oxygen they needed to keep race conflict smoldering.

City leaders abdicated control to lawyers, judges and outside experts and consultants.

There was a complete disconnect between the actual riot and the solutions to "unrest." And by taking the politically correct route of pretending mindless crime was actually a legitimate protest, the "root-cause" remedies let everyone off the hook to avoid addressing problems. Ultimately, Cincinnati handed off the megaphone to people who didn't even want it—the drug thugs and rioters.

The politicians outsourced the solutions. City council and the mayor never took ownership of the riot aftermath. Instead, they dumped the "solutions" on the courts and "experts."

Even if the critics were right, bringing in outsiders to reform the Cincinnati Police was a mistake, like trying to reform the Marine Corps with experts from the Salvation Army. It was exactly the wrong answer for a close-knit, proud organization like CPD.

Fred Siegel, who wrote the modern book on riots and cities, *The Future Once Happened Here*, said the Cincinnati response was unfortunately typical. "Politically, it makes no sense for the mayor to take on these issues," he said.

Politicians instead usually succumb to "riot ideology," he said, the politically correct remedy for "root causes." As columnist John Leo described it, riot ideology "is the belief that all black grievances are legitimate and must be assuaged at all costs."

Siegel predicted early on that Cincinnati would give in to riot ideology at a time when other riot-scarred cities such as Los Angeles have finally learned to repudiate it and refuse to follow the path of appeasement, spending, programs and pointless "dialogue."

Siegel's latest book, *Prince of the City*, is about New York Mayor Rudy Guiliani. What set Guiliani apart, Siegel said, is that he "took on that culture in every way."

There was no Guiliani to take on the culture of appeasement in Cincinnati. The city was paralyzed by political correctness. A city that cannot even call a race riot a riot, but has to hide it in a brown paper bag labeled "unrest," is ill-equipped to face its own problems.

In *Darkness at Noon* by Arthur Koestler, interrogator Ivanoff tells the prisoner Rubishov about the modern Soviet definition of human ethics, which "starts from the basic principle that a collective aim justifies all means, and not only allows, but demands, that the individual should in every way be subordinated and sacrificed to the community—which may dispose of it as an experimentation rabbit or a sacrificial lamb."

The media and political leaders of Cincinnati likewise established a "collective aim" that justified all means to suppress dissent. Objections and criticism were shouted down, ostracized, censored or ignored—"subordinated and sacrificed to the community."

And that collective aim quickly became the politically correct and expedient one: Blame the cops. Appease the protesters.

Amazingly, nobody was killed in the long week of Cincinnati race riots in April 2001. Not even one bullet was fired by the Cincinnati Police.

But while media, politicians, lawyers, protesters, judges and local leaders were busy blaming the cops, the cops backed off and the killing of young black men by young black men exploded. After the riots it spread like a plague through the same neighborhoods where gangs in drooping prisoner pants and Jesse James bandanas burned shops and smashed windows with rocks, bricks and bullets.

The homicide rate skyrocketed. By 2002, it had hit 64, breaking a 15-year record, 60 percent higher than the pre-riot year 2000. By 2003, homicides were off the chart at 75. By 2005, the city had 79 homicides.

A city that averaged about 80 shootings a year before the riots averaged more than 350 a year by 2005. "It's not unusual to see five a night," said Dr. Jay Johannigman, director of the University Hospital Trauma Unit. "I've been to Iraq twice. And I come home to my own community, and some nights I see more violence in my own hometown."

In 458 BC, a city in peril turned to Cincinnatus for rescue. In 2001, his namesake city Cincinnati chose appeasement and turned its back on its own citizen-soldiers, the cops who were the city's only hope. The legacy of that decision is measured in collapsing population, boarded up businesses and the blood of hundreds of young black men killed in drug wars.

Other cities should hope and pray that Cincinnati is the last to make that mistake.

WDBZ talk-show host Lincoln Ware
(center) interviews Police Chief Thomas
Streicher at the scene of riots on April 11
as SWAT Officer John Mercado stands by
with an assault rifle. No lethal rounds were
fired by police during the riots.

WHERE ARE THEY NOW?

A tuxedo-black awning once dressed up Eighth Street in downtown Cincinnati. The simple script over the sidewalk spelled "Maisonette" like elegant gold cufflinks. But now the city's most famous restaurant is gone. The china, polished silver and precious oil paintings have been auctioned away. The unparalleled excellence that earned a five-star Michelin rating for 40-straight years is gone. The Maisonette, a tradition for generations of weddings, proms, anniversaries and celebrations, locked its doors for the week of the riots, and then locked them for good four years later in the summer of 2005.

Some blamed poor management, competition and changing dining habits. But the Maisonette also suffered with the city. The riots scared away regular customers from suburban neighborhoods such as Mason and Indian Hill. And as crime headlines increased, fewer came back. Convention visitors dried up, as groups canceled to posture for a boycott or stayed away because they had heard the city was unsafe. The Maisonette is not the only burned out bulb in the city lights. But it's one of the most obvious and painful reminders that some scars take a long time to heal and some things will never be the same again.

People moved on and changed, too. The same year the Maisonette went out of business, Mayor Charlie Luken decided he would not seek reelection. New Mayor Mark Mallory became the city's first black strong mayor in 2005, and immediately let it be known that he would support the police, hold the black community more accountable for cooperation and make crime a top priority.

Luken left City Hall quietly and took a job as a lobbyist for a Cleveland firm that works in the state capital, Columbus.

City Manager John Shirey was forced to resign immediately after the riots and moved back to California to become executive director of the California Redevelopment Association, an agency that promotes affordable housing.

Cecil Thomas, director of the Cincinnati Human Relations Commission during the riots, resigned in 2005 and successfully ran for City Council.

Councilman Jim Tarbell ran again twice and won re-election to City Council both times.

Alicia Reece ran for mayor in 2005 and lost in the primary. After entering the mayoral race, she was not eligible to return to council.

John Cranley modified his position to be more of a supporter of police and finished first in the council race in 2005, then immediately entered a race for Congress.

Police Officer Stephen Roach took a job with the Evendale Police Department in Hamilton County just outside the Cincinnati city limits. After stormy meetings and protests over his hiring, he became one of the top officers in Evendale, earning commendations and thank-you notes from citizens and fellow officers. In 2006, the federal investigation of Roach was finally closed. An assistant U.S. Attorney General said there was not evidence to prove he acted improperly in a "fast moving, inherently dangerous situation in a dark alley."

Police Chief Thomas Streicher stayed on and vowed to put off retirement for several years to prevent being replaced by a new outsider chief who would no longer have civil service protection and would be at the mercy of City Hall politics.

Capt. Paul Humphries and the SWAT Team members remained with the Cincinnati Police Division, although CPD lost many veteran officers to other departments after the riots. Former SWAT officer Eric Hall left CPD and went to work at the University of Cincinnati, where he coordinates emergency preparation.

Former Assistant Chief Ron Twitty was forced to retire.

Lincoln Ware continues his popular morning talk show on WDBZ ("Da Buzz"). WLW talk-show personality Bill Cunningham still does his daily afternoon show.

The Rev. Damon Lynch III ran for council twice. He was nearly elected in 2003, but lost ground and finished farther back in 2005. During his campaign he did not discuss his boycott or leadership of the Black

United Front.

The mother of Timothy Thomas, Angela Leisure, was named 2001 Person of the Year by the alternative paper *CityBeat*. She moved away from Cincinnati.

FOP President Keith Fangman stepped down and volunteered to return to a beat in Over-the-Rhine. He was elected vice president of the Ohio Fraternal Order of Police.

William Kirkland and Gen. Kabaka Oba of the Black Fist continued to heckle city council meetings and other public gatherings.

Justice Watch Director Michael Howard counsels resident ex-convicts to help them stay off the streets, and also attends community gatherings to speak up for personal responsibility and more accountability in the black community to stop the spread of crime.

Larry Beaupre, former editor of *The Cincinnati Enquirer*, whose Chiquita debacle left the paper with a leadership vacuum during the riots, was transferred to Gannett Corporate headquarters in 1998 where he was directed to teach other editors about ethics. He later sued Gannett and claimed he was a scapegoat.

Publisher Harry Whipple also resigned in 2003 and left the *Enquirer* for a job as president of a joint operating agency for two newspapers in Salt Lake City, Utah.

Lawyer Ken Lawson has had health problems but continues to practice as the pugnacious "Law Dog."

Four years after the riots, Police Chief Tom Streicher spent weeks visiting every police station roll call for every shift to encourage cops to be more aggressive and do the job they had pledged to do, without second thoughts and reservations. The slow-down was over. But as neighborhoods were overcome by spreading drug crime, citizens began to demand more police. City Council responded by undermining police morale. When the TV show COPS came to town, to film Cincinnati officers in action and show the hard work they were doing to protect the public, Council members told the COPS producers they didn't want them in town. And when citizens crowded a council meeting to urge council members to keep their promise to hire 70 more cops, Council members told the crowd the money had been spent on other priorities, such as the federal monitors' expense accounts.

Five years after the riots that rocked Cincinnati in 2001, the city was still dealing with the lingering aftereffects. But by 2006, voters had replaced anti-cop council members with a new team that pledged support for the police. Constant focus on race problems was finally replaced with fresh optimism that an expanded convention center and new housing, entertainment and restaurants on the river front would bring a revival of energy, tourism and downtown nightlife.

Cincinnati could make headlines again as America's "Comeback City."

 Peter Bronson has been a reporter, editor and columnist at weekly and daily newspapers in Michigan, Arizona and Ohio. He came to Ohio from the *Tucson Citizen* in Arizona to become editorial page editor at the *Cincinnati Enquirer* in 1992. Under his leadership the *Enquirer* editorial pages were judged best in Ohio four years in a row. In 2002 he left management and meetings behind to return to writing full time as a columnist at the *Enquirer*.

Bronson was born in Ann Arbor, Mich. in 1953 and grew up in East Lansing, Michigan., where he was a car-parker, pizza-maker, snow-plow driver, construction worker, hippie clothing store salesman and ditch digger before graduating from Michigan State University in 1978 with a degree in journalism, which has been even more useful than his certificate from bartending school.

He has served on a variety of non-profits as a volunteer and board member, including Casa de los Ninos in Tucson and the Children's Home of Northern Kentucky. He has been a frequent speaker and television panelist in Tucson and on "Hotseat" on WCPO in Cincinnati. He lives in Loveland, Ohio with his family and is active in his church.